BERLIOZ'S
REQUIEM

Oxford KEYNOTES
Series Editor   KEVIN BARTIG

Sergei Prokofiev's Alexander Nevsky
KEVIN BARTIG

Arvo Pärt's Tabula Rasa
KEVIN C. KARNES

Aaron Copland's Appalachian Spring
ANNEGRET FAUSER

Rodgers and Hammerstein's Carousel
TIM CARTER

Arlen and Harburg's Over the Rainbow
WALTER FRISCH

Beethoven's Symphony No. 9
ALEXANDER REHDING

Claude Debussy's Clair de Lune
GURMINDER KAUR BHOGAL

Brian Eno's Ambient 1: Music for Airports
JOHN T. LYSAKER

Alfred Schnittke's Concerto Grosso no. 1
PETER J. SCHMELZ

George Bizet's Carmen
NELLY FURMAN

Jean Sibelius's Violin Concerto
TINA K. RAMNARINE

Puccini's La Bohème

ALEXANDRA WILSON

Antonín Dvořák's New World Symphony

DOUGLAS W. SHADLE

Beethoven's String Quartet in C-sharp Minor, Op. 131

NANCY NOVEMBER

Gioachino Rossini's The Barber of Seville

HILARY PORISS

Laurie Anderson's Big Science

S. ALEXANDER REED

Shostakovich's Symphony No. 5

MARINA FROLOVA-WALKER & JONATHAN WALKER

Manuel de Falla's El amor brujo

CAROL A. HESS

Berlioz's Requiem

JENNIFER WALKER

Oxford KEYNOTES

BERLIOZ'S *REQUIEM*

JENNIFER WALKER

Oxford University Press is a department of the University of Oxford. It furthers
the University's objective of excellence in research, scholarship, and education
by publishing worldwide. Oxford is a registered trade mark of Oxford University
Press in the UK and in certain other countries.

Published in the United States of America by Oxford University Press
198 Madison Avenue, New York, NY 10016, United States of America.

© Oxford University Press 2025

All rights reserved. No part of this publication may be reproduced, stored
in a retrieval system, transmitted, used for text and data mining, or used
for training artificial intelligence, in any form or by any means, without
the prior permission in writing of Oxford University Press, or as expressly
permitted by law, by licence or under terms agreed with the appropriate
reprographics rights organization. Enquiries concerning reproduction
outside the scope of the above should be sent to the Rights Department,
Oxford University Press, at the address above.

You must not circulate this work in any other form
and you must impose this same condition on any acquirer

Library of Congress Cataloging-in-Publication Data
Names: Walker, Jennifer (Jennifer P.) author.
Title: Berlioz's *Requiem* / Jennifer Walker.
Description: [1.] | New York, NY : Oxford University Press, 2025. |
Series: Oxford keynotes series |
Includes bibliographical references and index.
Identifiers: LCCN 2024058382 (print) | LCCN 2024058383 (ebook) |
ISBN 9780197688816 (paperback) | ISBN 9780197688809 (hardback) |
ISBN 9780197688847 | ISBN 9780197688823 (epub)
Subjects: LCSH: Berlioz, Hector, 1803-1869. Grande Messe des morts.
Classification: LCC ML410.B5 W25 2025 (print) | LCC ML410.B5 (ebook) |
DDC 782.32/38—dc23/eng/20241204
LC record available at https://lccn.loc.gov/2024058382
LC ebook record available at https://lccn.loc.gov/2024058383

DOI: 10.1093/9780197688847.001.0001

Series Editor's
INTRODUCTION

O XFORD KEYNOTES REIMAGINES THE canons of Western music for the twenty-first century. With each of its volumes dedicated to a single composition or album, the series provides an informed, critical, and provocative companion to music as artwork and experience. Books in the series explore how works of music have engaged listeners, performers, artists, and others through history and in the present. They illuminate the roles of musicians and musics in shaping Western cultures and societies, and they seek to spark discussion of ongoing transitions in contemporary musical landscapes. Each approaches its key work in a unique way, tailored to the distinct opportunities that the work presents. Targeted at performers, curious listeners, and advanced undergraduates, volumes in the series are written by expert and engaging voices in their fields, and will therefore be of significant interest to scholars and critics as well.

In selecting titles for the series, Oxford Keynotes balances two ways of defining the canons of Western music: as lists of works that critics and scholars deem to have articulated key moments in the history of the art, and as lists of works that comprise the bulk of what consumers listen to, purchase, and perform today. Often, the two lists intersect, but the overlap is imperfect. While not neglecting the first, Oxford Keynotes gives considerable weight to the second. It confronts the musicological canon with the living repertoire of performance and recording in classical, popular, jazz, and other idioms. And it seeks to expand that living repertoire through the latest musicological research.

Kevin Bartig
Michigan State University

CONTENTS

ACKNOWLEDGMENTS   xi

LIST OF ABBREVIATIONS   xv

Introduction   1

1. Hearing the *Requiem* in 1837   8
2. Berlioz and the Aesthetics of Sacred Music   28
3. Experiencing the *Requiem*: Berlioz and the Sacred Sublime   45
4. Building the *Requiem*: Berlioz as Aural Architect   77
5. Rehearing the *Requiem*   101

ADDITIONAL SOURCES FOR READING AND LISTENING   109

NOTES   113

INDEX   123

ACKNOWLEDGMENTS

T HIS BOOK BEGAN ITS life as a paper that I prepared for a conference, "Berlioz et Paris," held in 2019 in honor of the 150th anniversary of Berlioz's death. A surprise hospitalization prevented me from presenting my work, learning from colleagues, and enjoying Paris as one should, but the seed for this book had already started to sprout. Kevin Bartig, the editor of the Oxford Keynotes series, nurtured its growth and has enthusiastically supported the book from start to finish.

I am equally grateful to other colleagues, friends, and mentors who offered substantive feedback and collegial advice even after hearing me talk about Berlioz for what likely seemed an eternity. My gratitude is primarily due to Annegret Fauser for the selfless sharing of her time as I shared (very) rough drafts and unformed thoughts. She is an unparalleled mentor and friend. As I worked on another Berlioz project, Francesca Brittan and Sarah Hibberd offered deeply thoughtful insights that eventually found their way into this text, and I am likewise grateful to this book's anonymous readers, whose penetrating commentary was equal parts exacting and beneficial. Norm Hirschy and his colleagues at Oxford University Press shepherded the book over the finish line. Portions of this research were presented at numerous venues, including the Allegheny chapter and national meetings of the American Musicological Society, gatherings of the France: Musiques, Cultures network, and the Résonances Gothiques/Gothic Resonances conference in Avignon. I am especially grateful to the organizers and attendees of these meetings for their intuitive feedback. Research for this book was made possible through a fellowship from the West Virginia Humanities Council, a state affiliate of the National Endowment for the Humanities. Financial support was also generously offered during my year as a Humanities Center Fellow at the West Virginia University Humanities Center (2023–2024); grants given by the WVU College of Creative Arts also allowed me the necessary time and funding for research and writing. A simple thank you to each of these parties does not seem adequate.

Numerous friends and colleagues obliged my Berlioz obsession from near and far. To Jamie Blake and Imani Mosley, thank you for your help in acquiring materials that were not readily accessible to me. The West Virginia University School of Music provided my research assistant, Andrew Simonette, the financial support to assist me in some of the more tedious aspects of data collection. The occupants of the fourth floor "party hallway" offices at WVU—Katelyn Best, Eftihia Arkoudis, Matthew Heap, Jake Sandridge, and Alan Hankers—offered friendship, support, and laughter when I needed it most; Matt very kindly and patiently answered my numerous questions when it came to setting some of the musical examples, and

Erin Maher completed the index. Travis Stimeling, my colleague, mentor, close friend, and an honorary occupant of the party hallway, provided the perfect balance of straight-talking advice and genuine encouragement.

In February 2023, my family grew by one after my husband and I finalized the adoption of our nine-year-old son. I owe the largest debt of gratitude to my family, who spent countless afternoons and evenings occupying themselves while I completed this book, and I happily foresee countless hours of playing outside and ice cream cones. I dedicate this book to my son, Marley, with my unending love, and also to Travis Stimeling, whose sudden and unexpected death occurred after the completion of this text. Though they did not live to see this book published, their memory lives on through it. When the inevitable challenges involved in writing a book surfaced, Travis's kind spirit, selfless encouragement, and unflagging support made them seem inconsequential. Academia was a kinder place with Travis in it, and their memory shall remain a blessing to all who knew them.

ABBREVIATIONS

AHAP   Archives historiques de l'Archevêché de Paris

BoM   Katherine Kolb, *Berlioz on Music: Selected Criticism 1824–1837*. Translated by Samuel N. Rosenberg. New York: Oxford University Press, 2015.

BnF   Bibliothèque nationale de France

CG   Hector Berlioz, *Correspondance générale*. Edited by Pierre Citron et al. 8 vols. Paris: Flammarion, 1975.

CM   Hector Berlioz, *La Critique musicale d'Hector Berlioz*. Edited by H. Robert Cohen, Yves Gérard, Anne Bongrain, and Marie-Hélène Coudroy-Saghaï. 10 vols. Paris: Buchet/Chastel, 1996.

Memoirs   Hector Berlioz, *The Memoirs of Hector Berlioz*. Translated by David Cairns. New York: W. W. Norton, 1969.

MémoiresB   Hector Berlioz, *Mémoires d'Hector Berlioz de 1803 à 1865 et ses voyages en Italie, en Allemagne, en Russie et en Angleterre écrits par lui-même*. Edited by Peter Bloom. Paris: J. Vrin, 2019.

NBE 9	Hector Berlioz, *Grande Messe des morts.* In *Hector Berlioz: New Edition of the Complete Works.* Vol. 9. Edited by Jürgen Kindermann. Kassel: Bärenreiter, 1978.
NBE 24	Hector Berlioz, *Grand traité d'instrumentation.* In *Hector Berlioz: New Edition of the Complete Works.* Vol. 24. Edited by Peter Bloom. Kassel: Bärenreiter, 2003.
Nouvelles lettres	Peter Bloom, Joël-Marie Fauquet, Hugh J. Macdonald, and Cécile Reynaud, eds. Nouvelles lettres de Berlioz, de sa famille, de ses contemporains. Arles: Actes Sud/Palazzetto Bru Zane, 2016.
Treatise	Hector Berlioz, *Grand traité d'instrumentation et d'orchestration modernes.* Paris: Schonenberger, 1844.

INTRODUCTION

THE GEMSTONES AND THE REQUIEM

The first episode of HBO's *The Righteous Gemstones* (2019) opens in hour seventeen of a twenty-four-hour-long baptism marathon. The Gemstones, a family of megachurch-based televangelists, have taken their mission to China and are knee-deep in a pool that has become a sacramental assembly line. One by one, the male-identifying Gemstones baptize those who have waited patiently for their turn. An argument on how to properly immerse congregants soon breaks out between Jesse Gemstone, the eldest son, and Kelvin, his immature younger brother, and the baptismal "ceremony" quickly devolves into splash-filled petulance. Suddenly, we hear a mechanical buzzing. Baptizer and baptized are surprised by the sudden onslaught of waves: the

Berlioz's Requiem. Jennifer Walker, Oxford University Press. © Oxford University Press 2025.
DOI: 10.1093/9780197688847.003.0001

baptismal font is but the public wave pool. Chaos ensues—sacrament becomes pandemonium as strobe lights begin to flash over thumping rave music—and we, the audience, are fully brought into the show's quirky comedy and darkly amusing irreverence.

As the title screen emerges, a neon cross overlaid with "The Righteous Gemstones" comes into view. The image, emblazoned in all its Las Vegas–style illumined glory, slowly fills the screen, and the opening measures of the Rex tremendae from Hector Berlioz's *Requiem* (*Grande Messe des morts*, 1837) blast forth. As the episode progresses, the Gemstones return to their over-the-top homes and their criminal activities and we, the viewing audience, quickly learn that their external displays of Christian faith are flimsy façades that do little to obscure their opulent, greedy, arrogant, and often felonious lifestyles. How sincere the Gemstones are in their religious beliefs and practice is, to put it mildly, questionable: they are more concerned with their excessively shallow external appearances than they are with supporting their religious brand with any sort of actual belief.

The strains of "Rex!" heard in tandem with the gaudily incandescent cross quickly sparked interest among fans of *The Righteous Gemstones* as numerous Reddit users tried in vain to identify the music's source. While some identified it as having been written by Wolfgang Amadeus Mozart—described in one post as "this random guy from like the revolutionary war or something"—only a handful correctly recognized the music as having been written by Berlioz.[1] The show's critique of American megachurch culture and its questioning of religious sincerity writ large is obvious;

why a brief snippet from Berlioz's *Requiem* would underscore the series' titular and most recognizable visual image is perhaps less readily so. Why might the show's musical directors have chosen the *Requiem* as the most suitable sonic accompaniment for an image that visually represents the eponymous family's larger-than-life excess and feigned religious devotion?

Berlioz's critics often point to a perceived taint of excess in his music, whether it manifests as overt programmaticism (*Symphonie fantastique*, 1830), innovative, experimental, or even imitative orchestrational effects (the Hostias in the *Requiem*), or large-scale, so-called "monumental" works (the *Requiem* and the *Te Deum*, 1855). There remains, as Jacques Barzun so aptly noted in 2003, a "Berlioz problem."[2] The problem itself stems from a two-pronged historiographical narrative that continues to shape how we think about Berlioz's music. Berlioz reception is often treated in biohermeneutic, life-and-works terms; this type of approach is understandable after even a cursory scan of his memoirs. But while this sort of life-and-works approach is often appealing to concert audiences, it has also led to an uncritical acceptance of Berlioz as the excessive Romantic in terms that follow common preconceptions of Romantic music as emotionally expressive and boundary-pushing in form and scope.[3] Descriptors of Berlioz's music as wayward, unconventional, eccentric, and wild are often paired with similar portrayals of the composer as a "fervent reactionary" and a "passionate idealist"; in the words of the conductor Sir Colin Davis, he was "the first genuine Romantic, maybe the *only* genuine Romantic."[4] Often, there is thus an uneasy hesitance in critical approvals of Berlioz's music.

If Berlioz's excess or "originality" is viewed favorably, it is largely done so only in the service of situating it at the apex of nineteenth-century Romanticism. This approach is also not without some merit. The prominent nineteenth-century journal *Revue et Gazette musicale de Paris*, for example, devoted a significant portion of its coverage to Berlioz's music, and its early columns on the subject clearly situated the composer within a French Romantic framework.[5] And if, for example, the critic Oscar Comettant could write after Berlioz's death in 1869 that he would remain "one of the boldest personalities of the romantic school of music" regardless of his assessment that "his whole life was a fight for the triumph of a musical poetics of which we can disapprove," the Berlioz scholar Peter Bloom could echo the same sentiment in the twentieth century. Bloom argues that "what one can say without controversy is that the *Requiem* has become a symbol—like the tri-colored flag, and the Panthéon—of the one church of which Berlioz was more than a sometimes member, and that is the common church of flamboyance."[6]

The charge of overblown Romantic excess is even more pronounced when it comes to Berlioz's sacred music, for this charge also brings with it the perception of insincerity. Indeed, the theme of empty artifice disguised as Christian ritual that is so prevalently featured in *The Righteous Gemstones* is equally ubiquitous in the contemporary reception and understanding of the *Requiem*. Berlioz, of course, is partly to blame in this regard; though the opening paragraphs of his memoirs document an enjoyably Catholic childhood, his later indifference to organized religion is well documented. And yet there remains a pervasive belief that for Berlioz to have been a successful composer of sacred music he must also have been a devoutly practicing Catholic. For Paul Henry Lang, an American musicologist and music critic, Berlioz was the very "antithesis of a church composer" with "no understanding of things spiritual" and an "incapacity for meditation." The *Requiem* was, as a result, "altogether outside the pale of church music"; it was "purely dramatic and entirely removed from the liturgic."[7] Others have taken a softer tack and have worked to reconcile Berlioz's personal belief system with his sacred musical works. Writers often attempt to pinpoint the sources of a perceived spirituality in these works, yet even then, their assessments are laden with implicit accusations of insincerity. One scholar, for example, has described the *Requiem*, the *Te Deum*, and *L'Enfance du Christ* (1854) as products of a biohermeneutic "artistic religiosity" that is secular in overall conception but sacred in expression and tone.[8] Another has gone so far to suggest that, as far as Berlioz is concerned, the label of "sacred music" is inaccurate and that a more precise descriptor in this case might be "works based on liturgical texts and subjects."[9] Berlioz thus seems to be lacking in sincerity—an essential element in the composition of appropriately sacred music. That Devoe Yates, the musical supervisor for *The Righteous Gemstones*, chose the opening of the Rex tremendae for such a specific visual moment in show's opening is therefore unsurprising. Berlioz's *Requiem* is a large work—a performance that adheres to Berlioz's exacting prescriptions requires upward of three hundred musicians—and the first bars of the Rex tremendae are some of the largest-scale moments of the entire work. Berlioz calls for the full battery of his orchestra, including eight timpani and four supplemental brass orchestras that burst forth in the full *fortissimo* statement of "Rex!" Where Yates could have chosen any other moment from the *Requiem* (or, indeed, from any other composer's setting of the requiem mass), he carefully chose one in which Berliozian excess, theatricality, and alleged insincerity was on full display, arguably as a musical complement to the profligacy of the neon cross and the similarly empty excess and insincerity that it represents.

This book seeks to move modern hearings and understandings of the *Requiem* beyond the confines of Gemstone-style dramatics and theatricality. If audiences and scholars are often left puzzling over the conundrum of Berlioz's sacred works, the chapters in this book aim to fill in the missing pieces. Beginning with a brief overview of the work's genesis and premiere, the discussion moves into a detailed account of the *Requiem*'s immediate reception—what, if anything, did listeners and critics find to be notable? The following chapter explores how Berlioz's nineteenth-century listeners would have listened to and heard the work by exploring how Berlioz understood sacred music and how he thought it should sound. After the second chapter, the focus shifts to how we, as today's listeners, might rehear the *Requiem*. The remaining chapters unravel the musical, theological, and cultural contexts that allowed Berlioz's own audiences to hear the work in ways that push beyond the bounds of theatricality and drama. Whether through concert performances around the globe or through *The Righteous Gemstones*, the *Requiem* has garnered a distinctive place in the contemporary auditory imagination. If we are to move past hearing and understanding the *Requiem* as an icon of Romanticism and of religious indifference, then we must look farther than the flashy world of the Gemstones or the attractively sensational narrative of nineteenth-century Romanticism. In doing so, we might hear the *Requiem* anew.

CHAPTER 1
HEARING THE REQUIEM IN 1837

I shall undoubtedly bring upon myself the reproach of *innovation* once more because I wanted to return this area of art to a *truth* from which Mozart and Cherubini seem to me to have strayed too often. Then there are some startling combinations which, I'm happy to say, have never been tried before and about which, I think, I had the first idea.[1]

On a warm summer afternoon in late July 1835, the French king, Louis-Philippe, paraded down the Boulevard du Temple with his royal entourage. Accompanied by three of his sons, the Duke of Orleans, the Duke of Nemours, and the Prince de Joinville, the king processed as part of an annual review of the national guard that commemorated the 1830 July Revolution. This was the first of the occasions celebrating the *Trois glorieuses*—the three days in July 1830

Berlioz's Requiem. Jennifer Walker, Oxford University Press. © Oxford University Press 2025.
DOI: 10.1093/9780197688847.003.0002

that marked the conciliation of the republican factions with the constitutional monarchists, the abdication of Charles X, and the proclamation of Louis-Philippe as king. Ironic, yes—for the street down which the king and his retinue filed was itself full of revolutionary symbolism: the Boulevard du Temple connects the Place de la République to the Bastille.

A revolutionary cause appeared in another guise as the procession continued along its route. At number 50 Boulevard du Temple, Giuseppe-Maria Fieschi and a band of radical accomplices lay in wait for the royal cortège. As the party passed on the street below, Fieschi opened fire with a homemade gun equipped with over twenty barrels rigged to fire at once: his so-called infernal machine. Though Fieschi missed his mark—Louis-Philippe survived with only minor wounds, famously commanding his troops "*Messieurs, continuons!*"—eighteen people died at his hands. Among the dead were high-ranking members of the royal staff, including the king's commander-in-chief, the Maréchal de France Édouard-Adolphe Mortier.

Some months later, in March 1837, the national government invited Hector Berlioz, the then thirty-four-year-old composer, to compose a requiem mass for Mortier and the other victims of Fieschi's rampage. Berlioz was not an unlikely choice. Having already made a name for himself as a composer, he was a known quantity with both critics and audiences. He was also known for his work as a music critic, and his close association with the Bertin family (the owners of the widely read *Journal des débats*, a publication for which Berlioz wrote for thirty years) brought with it a certain proximity to Louis-Philippe and the centers of power during the July Monarchy. The request for a requiem that would itself commemorate a commemoration of the *Trois glorieuses* likewise fit him well. He supported the July Monarchy and the overthrow of Charles X, and as he told it, he found himself swept away from composing music into the middle of the breathless revolution:

> It was the year 1830. I was finishing my cantata [*Sardanapale*] when the Revolution broke out. Grapeshot rattled on the barricaded doors, cannon-balls thudded against the façade, women screamed, and in the brief lulls in the firing, the swallows filled the air with their shrill sweet cry.
>
> I dashed off the final pages of my orchestral score to the sound of stray bullets coming over the roofs and pattering on the wall outside my window. On [July] 29th I had finished and was free to go out and roam about Paris till morning, pistol in hand.

"And the music that was there, then," he recounted, "the songs . . . nobody who did not hear it can have any idea what it was like."[2] Berlioz's penchant for hyperbolic reminiscences aside, the 1830 Revolution cemented Berlioz's patriotism. The opportunity to musically memorialize the victims of an attempt on the livelihood of the monarchical lineage was welcome and his new requiem mass might, as he wrote to his mother, "become the property of the nation."[3]

Berlioz received the commission to compose the *Requiem* from the minister of the interior, the Comte Adrien de Gasparin; it was to be ready for performance at the church of Saint-Louis-des-Invalides, the official chapel of French military services, on July 28, 1837. The commission, however, had been months in the making. Earlier in 1836, Gasparin proposed that three thousand francs be set aside out of the reserves of the Department of Fine Arts for the composition of a "large-scale mass or oratorio by a French composer" who would be personally nominated by the minister. This was, according to Berlioz, the result of the minister's desire to "restore sacred music to the prestige which it had long ago lost in France." As Berlioz remembered it, Gasparin considered him to be perfect person for the job: "I shall begin with Berlioz," he declared. "He ought to write a Requiem Mass. I am sure he will do it well."[4]

Having heard of the high esteem in which Gasparin held his work from a friend of a friend, Berlioz requested a personal audience with the minister to confirm for himself that which he had only heard through the grapevine. Gasparin was nearing the end of his tenure in the Ministry, and he seemed surprised to hear that Berlioz had not yet received the official commission. Citing bureaucratic oversight, Gasparin claimed that the commission should have arrived the week prior. It had not, and later conversations would reveal that Edmond Cavé, the director of fine arts, did not support Gasparin's initiative to encourage the composition of new sacred music. Even less so did he agree with his ministerial colleague that Berlioz was the right person for the job. Cavé preferred Rossini to Berlioz and was no fan of what he considered to be the "avant-garde."[5] Postponing the minister's request for a drafted commission meant that, at least for Cavé, the delay would coincide with Gasparin's last days in office and that, following the installation of the new minister, the idea and Berlioz's commission could be quashed altogether. Luigi Cherubini, Cavé's personal choice, could then be given the commission that some felt he rightly deserved. Berlioz's account tells us the minister's sharply worded demand that Cavé draft and send the commission was successful at the eleventh hour: it was, according to Berlioz, "duly done," and he was to receive a sum of four thousand francs for his labor.[6]

Berlioz's delayed receipt of the commission was only the beginning of a series of logistic and bureaucratic missteps. After having worked in a self-described state of fury in which his "brain felt as though it would explode," he completed the score on June 29, 1837. Berlioz demanded a massive bloc of musicians for the performance. Five hundred performers, including two hundred singers, borrowed from the Paris Opéra and the church choirs of Saint-Eustache and La Madeleine, had already started rehearsing, the Opéra's professional copyist was engaged to begin the monumental (and expensive) task of copying the orchestral and choral parts, and the construction of a wooden platform to accommodate the performers was in full swing. And suddenly the performance was canceled without a hint of warning. Perhaps the cancellation was the result of a financial shortfall: budgets were tight following the massive costs incurred by the recent wedding of the Duke of Orleans to Princess Hélène of Mecklenburg. It is possible that the ceremony was canceled for political reasons; the three-day ceremony had been shortened to one. Perhaps the change was the product of Cavé's documented disdain for both Gasparin and Berlioz or even Cherubini's hostility at having been passed over. For whatever reason, the *Requiem* was left unheard, and Berlioz was left unpaid and saddled with the debt that he had personally incurred in preparation for the premiere.[7] Such was a blow that was, for Berlioz, "enough to make one snort like a whale."[8]

Berlioz spent the following few months arguing in vain with the government for his promised payment. He could not foresee that October would bring a new occasion for the performance of his *Requiem*. On October 13, the French captured Constantine in what became the early stages of the French colonialist domination of northern Africa. Three days later, as Berlioz returned home from a contentious meeting with Cavé, the clanging bells of the Invalides chapel signaled the news that the commanding general and governor-general of Algeria, Charles-Marie Denys, comte de Damrémont, had been killed in the siege. The city of Paris prepared itself for yet another period of official mourning. A grand ceremony was once again in order, and Berlioz seized the chance to have his requiem mass performed. He urged his supporters to petition government ministries on his behalf; word came in early November of their success:

> Yesterday the two Ministers (of the Interior and of War) finally signed the decree that designates my *Requiem* for the <u>funeral service</u> for General Damrémont. I fought hard for a week to obtain the sum I need, and now I have it, at least in the form of an official promise. The Minister of War is granting *10,000 francs* for the performance, and the Minister of the Interior is taking responsibility for the payment of the *8,700 francs* that are owed to me for the composition, copying, and rehearsals done in July. This does not prevent them from making cruel cuts to my orchestra and chorus, so that instead of 400 musicians I will only have a total of 270 men, women, and children.[9]

Given that Damrémont had fallen in active combat, the Ministry of War—with its deep pockets—was now responsible for funding the funeral ceremony. Though Berlioz recouped his July losses (though not until early 1838), he was not paid the full sum, and the smaller payment left him lacking in the number of performers that he was able to have at his disposal; they were reduced from the original five hundred to under three hundred.[10] Nearly half a year following the completion of the score, the *Requiem* was heard for the first time as General Damrémont was laid to rest.

DECEMBER 5, 1837

The chapel of the Invalides was cloaked in partial darkness. The grand windows were hung with heavy black drapes and what little lighting shone through left the space in semi-obscurity. Battle flags riddled with bullet holes swayed back and forth. The church doors opened at ten o'clock in the morning for attendees who had tickets. One hour later, the solemn procession began. Members of the Ministry of Public Instruction, the Prefect of the Seine, the Prefecture of the Police, and members of the municipal council of Paris entered and were seated on the right side of the dome; on the left were members of the diplomatic corps and high-ranking members of the military. The right and left sides of the nave were reserved for the musicians— five hundred of them by one account—and fifty places were reserved for the leaders of the national guard and other military officials. The ceremony began at noon. The royal family entered to the sound of military drums and seven cannon blasts: the Duc d'Orléans appeared first, followed closely by the Duc d'Aumale and the Duc de Montpensier, who processed down the main aisle and were received by members of the clergy and government ministries. Under the chapel's vast dome lay an imposing catafalque atop which the casket rested. Four lieutenant-generals were stationed at each of the casket's corners, and the family of the fallen general were seated close by.[11] The mass then began in force, celebrated by the priest of the Invalides chapel; the absolution was said by the Archbishops of Paris, Nancy, Marseille, and Saint-Flour. It was a "solemn spectacle" worthy of all the dignity warranted by the occasion. One writer vividly described the solemnity of the visual experience:

> Somber draperies lined with six thousand candles, these sparkling chandeliers, this funeral altar, this catafalque loaded with luminaries and glorious emblems, those conquered arms that rise in beams, shields, yataghans . . . these floating flags, these old soldiers who guard them, and at the top of your head, across the lamps' smoke, the dome of the Invalides, softly lit by a timid sunbeam that seems to give life and movement to this tableau of eternal resurrection—it is undoubtedly a sclemn spectacle.[12]

The grandeur of the funereal paraphernalia in the Invalides might well have been supplemented—perhaps even subsumed—by the sight of a massive choral and orchestral ensemble, spread on either side of the organ, meticulously situated on risers, with its corners flanked by separate brass choirs. The raft of musicians included a tenor soloist, eighty sopranos, sixty tenors, seventy basses, fifty violins, eighteen double basses, twelve trumpets, sixteen trombones, eight pairs of timpani, four brass choirs that included multiple ophicleides, and additional ranks of percussion. The performers were among the best that Paris had to offer. François-Antoine Habeneck, *premier chef* at the Paris Opéra and the founder of the Société des Concerts du Conservatoire, conducted an orchestra that was composed of top students and players from the city's finest ensembles. The chorus, led by Jean Schneitzhoeffer, the *chef de chant* at the Opéra, included such operatic stars as Nicolas-Prosper Levasseur, Alexis Dupont, Adolphe-Joseph-Louis Alizard, and Rosine Stoltz. The celebrated tenor Gilbert Duprez sang the solo in the Sanctus. It was massive, grand, monumental; to some, even dramatic. Expectations were high.

"In the sad and glorious ceremony of this day, art came to religion's aid to celebrate the general of Constantine and the brave dead with him," wrote one unnamed observer in the widely read *Journal des débats*.[13] Art, in this case, was Berlioz's musical setting of the Catholic mass for the dead: the aural experience of Damrémont's funeral was crowned by the sounds of Berlioz's *Requiem*. The city was anxious to hear the requiem mass that had been billed as the artistic high point of the day's solemn events, and curiosities abounded. Advance press notices reported that Berlioz had demanded upward of five hundred musicians for the performance and required a special scaffolding that could accommodate the massive choir and orchestra. Was Berlioz successful? Did the *Requiem* meet the public's expectations? What did the audience at the Invalides hear on that December afternoon?

The performance was, in Berlioz's words, a great success: it was "perfect [. . .] a success immense and general with artists as with the public."[14] There were, of course, those who disagreed with Berlioz's assessment. A writer identified as X. Y. Z. railed against Berlioz and his newest work. Writing in *Le Constitutionnel*, a newspaper that was often deeply critical of the Catholic church, the critic claimed that "if the thought that dictated these homages to our army's bravery and to its leader's devotion is great and national . . . we must admit that the performance offered nothing remarkable, including Berlioz's mass." He drew a comparison between Berlioz's *Requiem* and the "great" Requiems by François-Joseph Gossec, Wolfgang Amadeus Mozart, and Cherubini. While he was able to admit that the performance itself was noteworthy, the critic quipped that it was only made so by a "religiously attentive audience wholly ready to let their emotions go." Taken in its entirety, he wrote, the *Requiem* was disjointed, harsh, and full of short bursts of true inspiration that fizzled out as quickly as they began. The supplementary brass ensembles, for example, were not heard as a homogeneous part of the larger ensemble. They were instead tacked on as an afterthought and were thought of only as a necessity given the nature of the military funeral. And while the author found something in the Agnus Dei that warranted genuine praise—"a very beautiful melody"—he nonetheless was convinced that this small portion of the work would have been the part with which Berlioz was the least satisfied. "He must have considered it as a sacrifice to the taste of the vulgar," he wrote. "Berlioz is very much more struck by certain effects of piccolos and serpents that call to each other with the sharpest and deepest notes than by all the melody in his Agnus Dei." The De profundis, chanted at the Archbishop of Paris's request after the conclusion of the *Requiem*, was thought to be a better performance than all the *Requiem* combined.[15] And later, on December 7, another writer, whose scorn for Berlioz and the *Journal des débats* was plain, inaccurately quipped that "all the editors at the *Journal des débats* have the cross of honor except for Berlioz, but he will have it; they have already paid him 28,000 francs for a musical mass that is not worth one hundred crowns."[16]

Though it was plain that the critic X. Y. Z. had an axe to grind (he noted his disdain at Berlioz's famous dislike of the opera *Zampa* and his critical treatment of its composer, Ferdinand Herold), he was not alone in his biting critique— yet he was easily in the minority. Berlioz reported that the Duke of Orleans was deeply moved by the performance, and the priest of the Invalides, Abbé Ancelin, was apparently moved to tears—so much so that he remained weeping in the sacristy after the performance ended.[17] The minister of war, General Simon Bernard, wrote to Berlioz that "the success obtained by this beautiful and severe composition responded fittingly to the solemnity of the circumstance." He continued his praise of the *Requiem* by noting that the performance was a welcome opportunity to make his talent shine—a talent that ranked him at the top of composers of sacred music.[18] Bernard was not alone in his celebration of the *Requiem* as an exemplar of sacred music. One writer hailed it as "a masterwork worthy of being compared with the most celebrated inspirations of sacred music." Though a positive review might not have been wholly surprising from the *Journal des débats*, an anonymous writer nevertheless claimed that it "brings us back to the finest days of

Christian art when Christian art was the unique, patient, obstinate work of souls whom God had chosen for himself." And a critic writing for *Le Monde dramatique*, a journal whose founder was known for his affinity for French Romanticism, wrote not of the work's status as an emblem of Romanticism, but rather that, in the Sanctus, the "melody distinguishes itself through an entirely religious color, simultaneously noble and sad." This, however, was not all, for the work situated Berlioz at the apex of French sacred music. In *Le Charivari*, a publication known for its satirical bent, an anonymous writer wrote with surprising sincerity that "Berlioz's enemies must be silent and admire such a composition!"[19]

Critics and supporters of the *Requiem* at least agreed on the idea that its success depended largely on whether it was appropriately and genuinely religious. Engagement with the long-held critical chestnut that music set for liturgical purposes must necessarily sound a certain way—in a word, "sincere"—was at the heart of the matter. Therein lay the crux of what audiences expected from Berlioz, how they listened to what they heard at the premiere, and the ways in which those sounds were dissected and reviewed by the press soon thereafter. Joseph d'Ortigue, Berlioz's close friend and an erstwhile (if not overly conservative) champion of music for the church, looked forward to hearing the *Requiem* at long last. He had already railed against its earlier cancellation at the government's hands, for he saw Berlioz's commission to write a large-scale requiem as an encouragement to young artists who might have catalyzed the creation of a new national school of church music. D'Ortigue had not yet heard a note of Berlioz's new work, but in August 1837, he teased the public as to what they might have heard had the performance gone forward as originally planned:

This could be sublime; this could also be a mediocre thing. However, it is permissible to believe that the author of the *Marche au supplice*, the overture to [*Les*] *Francs-Juges*, and [*Le*] *Roi Lear* would rediscover his customary inspirations while treating an equally grand subject, that his imagination will be transported to the valley of Jehoshaphat, and that he will have seen all of humanity groaning and moaning there. It is permissible to believe that he will have penetrated the liturgical text's magnificent poetry and that he would have worked to reproduce the effect of these mournful plainchants and these terrible fauxbourdons that resonate in the church during the office of the dead.[20]

He had high hopes for Berlioz's *Requiem*, especially as they pertained to his own views on sacred music. D'Ortigue, who had so greatly anticipated hearing the *Requiem*, should have, at least in theory, been Berlioz's toughest critic when it came to writing music for the church. D'Ortigue was an Ultramontane Catholic critic who had already made a name for himself in the realm of sacred music, and though he and Berlioz were close friends, the two had vastly differing ideas about how sacred music should be composed and should sound. From the late 1820s, d'Ortigue published numerous essays in musical and religious journals that proclaimed medieval plainchant as the most appropriately sacred music. Its appeal, at least in his estimation, lay in its ease of communal performance and its similarities to God's "immutability, eternity, and infinity."[21] Berlioz's success would depend on a deep understanding of the liturgical text, a keen sense for how it should be treated musically, a sonic recreation of religious terror and sublime awe, and a faithful reproduction of plainchant and fauxbourdon—elements of the musical past that he believed to best embody the true essence of sacred music. That Berlioz was offered the commission in the first place and not Cherubini, who had recently completed his own requiem, spoke not only to his positive reputation, but also to the belief that Berlioz was up to the task.[22]

D'Ortigue was not alone in supporting Berlioz's credentials as a composer of sacred music. Following the 1827 performance of his *Messe solennelle*, for example, an unnamed critic in *Le Corsaire* lauded the young Berlioz for the care with which he had set the Mass. The virtue of Berlioz's writing stood in stark opposition to that of the "powerless harmonists" who were products of the Paris Conservatoire. Much as Berlioz himself would do, the writer protested the declining state of French sacred music. "Young men who devoted themselves to the god of harmony," he wrote, made their early marks through the composition of sacred music. Though sacred music used to provide the widest field of discovery for a young composer's imagination, the lack of church-based musical education—especially when coupled with the positivistic bent of the Conservatoire's teaching— was responsible for these "powerless harmonists."[23] Berlioz, however, was not to be confused with his classmates at the Conservatoire, for he had proven himself to be a "young virtuoso" with his *Messe solennelle*: indeed, the writer concluded his article by exhorting Berlioz not to remain at the Conservatoire—he was simply too good not to pursue a career devoted to the composition of sacred music. As a result, Berlioz's *Requiem* had the potential to be a great success. It might possibly even be sublime.

D'Ortigue began his lengthy review of the *Requiem* by expounding on the question of whether an artist or composer could create Christian art without themselves being Christian. A believing artist, he explained, could just as easily "ignore the conditions of religious art" as a non-believing one could possess the "secret of initiation." Mozart, he argued, was a "seriously religious man"—as was Beethoven—but their music made nothing but "monstrous amalgam[s] of worldly accents and holy words"; their juxtapositions of liturgical texts with "worldly" music committed the cardinal sin of juxtaposing the theater with the church. Of no matter to d'Ortigue was the question of whether Berlioz himself was truly religious or an actively practicing Catholic. What did matter was whether Berlioz's music was appropriately religious (at least, that is, according to d'Ortigue's standards). Whereas a writer for the widely read *Le Figaro* argued that the *Requiem*'s underlying fault was that it lacked "religious character" and Joseph Mainzer, an ordained priest and writer for *Le National*, took Berlioz to task for his liberal reworkings of the liturgical text, d'Ortigue disagreed. For the *Figaro* writer, the *Requiem*'s shortcomings—or perhaps even its lack of religious sincerity—were not so much the fault of liturgical reconfigurations (the writer cited the omission of the traditional Pie Jesu) but were instead the products of orchestrational excess or, as he put it, the "power of the serpent's bellowing and some rather multiplied blows on the tam-tam."[24] D'Ortigue, however, praised the "marvelous power with which [Berlioz] appropriated not only religious color, but even still the traditions of Christian art from the Middle Ages." The *Requiem* ran the stylistic gamut from what d'Ortigue described as "plainchants, fauxbourdons, counterpoint from the Middle Ages, the a cappella style, vocal fugue, instrumental fugue, orchestral music, and dramatic music." The Quaerens me was written in a "style alla Palestrina"; d'Ortigue heard the Offertoire as fauxbourdon. And yet the *Requiem*'s most dramatic parts—the Lacrymosa, according to d'Ortigue—were not enough so to overshadow the work's innately religious character.[25] Instead, the *Requiem* was perceived as truly religious by one of Paris's most conservatively Catholic critics by virtue of its proximity to medieval sacred music: plainchant, fauxbourdon, and the like. It was high praise indeed, for part of d'Ortigue's agenda in idealizing plainchant as sacred music was separating it from the Renaissance polyphony of Giovanni Luigi da Palestrina and his contemporaries. This distinction was important. Whereas Renaissance polyphony had been so tainted by the period's perceived anti-Catholic status that it could not be considered appropriately sacred, medieval plainchant was the product of an era that valued faith, piety, and simplicity. If Palestrina was "devoid of liturgical merit," chant and its corollaries (fauxbourdon) were pure, communal, and Christian.[26] Even if Berlioz's Quaerens me had been written in a quasi-Palestrinian style, the rest of the *Requiem*'s innately religious character remained intact by virtue of its proximity to musical styles that were understood as inviolately sacred. For d'Ortigue, the *Requiem* had shown its composer to be a "Catholic artist" who had followed the "rules of liturgy"—despite, of course, the fact that Berlioz had liberally reworked the liturgical text.[27]

D'Ortigue was not the only critic who responded in this way to the *Requiem*. Bottée de Toulmon, the librarian at the Paris Conservatoire, wrote an equally lengthy review in the influential *Revue et Gazette musicale de Paris* in which he likewise took up the task of defining what musical qualities could render a work either sacred or secular. He asked his readers to consider exactly what the difference between the two styles was in the first place. There was, in his mind, no distinguishable stylistic musical difference; the only difference to be found was in the text. What was it that had "distanced religious music from sources of true expression," and why, he asked, should composers and critics continue to separate the religious and the expressive? With the *Requiem*, however, "a musical work has suddenly arisen that is worthy of the epochs of fervor and belief, a work whose expression is so conscientious, so naively true, that we could imagine that it was born in the Middle Ages"—if, that is, the craft of Berlioz's formal construction and orchestration did not reveal itself to be modern. For Toulmon, the *Requiem* was unequivocally successful. There was no better musical expression of Christian thought and of the sacred sound world of the Middle Ages than the *Requiem*, for Berlioz had crafted an exact sonic reflection of the liturgical text.[28] An unsigned reviewer in the *Journal des débats* concurred. Though the writer did not specifically link the *Requiem* with the Middle Ages, they nonetheless praised Berlioz as embodying a specifically Christian past: it "brings us back to the finest days of Christian art when it was the unique, patient, and obstinate work of souls that God had chosen for himself."[29] D'Ortigue, too, found parts of the work to be evocative of a bygone Christianity. The Hostias, he wrote, reminded him of "sacred trumpets in funeral ceremonies and ancient mysteries." If Adolphe Boschot, an early twentieth-century music critic and significant (albeit cynical) Berlioz biographer, found the *Requiem*'s engagement with medievalist tropes to be evidence of the work's innate Romanticism, Berlioz's contemporaries praised it as emblematic of the Middle Ages—and this was enough to classify it as appropriately sacred.[30] Even d'Ortigue's brief mention of the Hostias as evocative of sacred trumpets and ancient mysteries lent credence to his positive assessment of the *Requiem* as a truly sacred musical work. Toulmon agreed. Berlioz had crafted a truly sacred work that was "most flattering for our national pride."

Listeners in 1837 expected to hear a work that engaged appropriately with their expectations of how sacred music should sound. Critics often argued about how those stylistic parameters should be defined, but Berlioz's *Requiem* was successful with the critics on largely all fronts; absent from the reception of the premiere was any sustained discussion of the *Requiem* as dramatic, grandiose, or Romantic. If some critics were dissatisfied with the work (X. Y. Z., for example), they occupied a small yet vocal minority. The minister of war was as pleased with the end result as he was with himself for having secured the commission in the first place: "this beautiful and severe composition responded to the solemnity of the event with dignity, and I applaud myself for having given you this new occasion to make the talent which places you in the first rank among our composers of sacred music shine."[31] Even the *Requiem*'s staunchest opponents conceded a certain proximity to sacred music. Mainzer's altogether negative review (unsurprising, given that it followed close on the heels of a recent falling out with Berlioz), focused almost entirely as it was on Berlioz's non-liturgical (or even anti-liturgical) adaptations of the text, situated the sound of the Hostias (the movement that later writers would single out as strange and eccentric) within the context of plain-chant. The trombone/flute pairing, for example, "always rendered the last sound of plainchant with a very suspicious humming."[32] But even Mainzer's comments focused on how the acoustic effect of the orchestration distorted a perceived likeness to plainchant, the sacred sound par excellence for numerous critics. At the premiere, then, critics were primarily interested in the work's status as sacred music. Toulmon's essay in the *Revue et Gazette musicale*, a journal whose early reviews of Berlioz's music were "unashamedly Romantic in tone," focused more on defending the *Requiem* as appropriately sacred than it did on whether Berlioz had composed another work that possessed characteristics that could be heard and understood as Romantic in nature. This critical trend continued in force throughout Berlioz's lifetime, and thus the *Requiem*'s value resided in how it could be heard, understood, and appreciated as genuinely religious: if critics writing in 1837 heard it as dramatic or theatrical, they rarely said so. Instead, the audience and the press focused their comments on the ways in which *Requiem* could (and should) be heard as an inherently sacred work. Like his critics, Berlioz had his own ideas about how sacred music could and should sound. Perhaps the question to ask, then, is this: why do many modern listeners hear the *Requiem* in such a different way? Unraveling Berlioz's idiosyncratic concept of sacred sound within the fabric of French sacred music may well provide the answer.

CHAPTER 2

BERLIOZ AND THE AESTHETICS OF SACRED MUSIC

We do not hesitate to affirm that Berlioz's *Requiem* marks a completely new era for sacred music: it now proves that there is a benefit in making reasoned expression succeed routine formula for the church's dignity.[1]

Berlioz found the state of sacred music in France during the early decades of the nineteenth century to be in a precariously rapid state of decline. Sacred music, for Berlioz, had a "sublime subject" and should inspire artistic creativity to the "acme of perfection."[2] Inspiration was lacking, however, and Berlioz was deeply interested in how it might be revived. His interest developed early. It was the occasion of his first communion, early on a bright and breezy spring morning. A young Berlioz, eager but nervous, waited among a group of girls, clad in white, for the priest's

Berlioz's Requiem. Jennifer Walker, Oxford University Press. © Oxford University Press 2025.
DOI: 10.1093/9780197688847.003.0003

summons to the altar. As he moved forward to receive the eucharist, he was overtaken by a rhapsodic sound:

> A chorus of fresh young voices broke into the eucharistic hymn. The sound filled me with a kind of mystical, passionate unrest which I was powerless to hide from the rest of the congregation. I saw Heaven open—a Heaven of love and pure delight, purer and a thousand times lovelier than the one that had so often been described to me. Such is the magic power of true expression, the incomparable beauty of melody that comes from the heart![3]

Some years later, while in Rome, an older Berlioz had a similar sonic experience while visiting Saint Peter's basilica:

> [I heard] a faint rumbling from some distant corner of the church, reverberating around the great vaults like far-off thunder. A sudden fear seized me. It seemed to me that this really was the temple of God, that I had no right to be here . . . and as I thought of the glorious role that my own art must play there, my heart began to beat with excitement.[4]

In the case of his first communion, the "eucharistic hymn" was neither plainchant nor motet: Berlioz identified it as the aria "Quand le bien-aimé reviendra" from Nicolas Dalayrac's opéra-comique *Nina* (1786), reset with a text suitable for the celebration of the eucharist. At the Sistine Chapel, Berlioz heard an unidentified "Miserere," likely Gregorio Allegri's, that he described as "music of the distant past which has come down to us unchanged in style or form."[5] These well-known episodes of sacred listening had a profound effect on his aesthetic ideologies when it came to his understanding and composition of sacred music. They also stand at odds with the indifference with which he came to view the Catholic Church. His early years were marked by a certain proximity to Catholicism, for he developed close friendships with deeply devout Catholics in Paris (Humbert Ferrand, Joseph d'Ortigue, and Princess Carolyne von Sayn-Wittgenstein), he published criticism in the Catholic press (e.g., the newspaper *Le Correspondant*), and his first large-scale work was a mass (*Messe solennelle*, 1825). And yet his later life was characterized by an abiding skepticism toward institutionalized religion and doctrinal praxis; he was, as David Cairns described it, "at pains to present himself as an unbeliever."[6] But even if Berlioz was not always a faithful Catholic in the traditional sense, sacred music remained a matter in which he was deeply invested throughout his career—indeed, his recollections of the *Requiem*'s genesis are couched in language that describes the genre of sacred music as one that had been neglected and had fallen from a former state of glory.[7] He thus worked diligently to ameliorate what he saw as a pressing musical crisis. For Berlioz, the solution was simple: expression and sincerity should work hand in hand to craft an aesthetic of sacred music that could resuscitate and transform a dying form of art.

SACRED MUSIC IN DECLINE

The French Catholic Church spent the early portion of the nineteenth century reeling from the aftereffects of the French Revolution, during which scores of church property were seized and clerical privileges suspended. As the Church and its supporters allied themselves with monarchists who worked toward restoring the monarchy and re-establishing the Church to its former power, other French intellectuals and politicians resisted the close alignment of the traditional Catholic Church with the French state. The Revolution had targeted any institution that was allied with the monarchy, and the closure and seizure of church property was disastrous for the composition of sacred music. Most, if not all, church choir schools (*maîtrises*) were closed in the wake of the monarchy's collapse in 1792. Interest in the grand motet, the favored genre of pre-Revolutionary sacred music composers, waned amid critical calls for a more diverse corpus of sacred music. In a post-Revolutionary context in which the state no longer controlled the composition of sacred music, newer religious works often took on the character of Revolutionary festivals: they were "grand in scale, simple in conception."[8] The 1801 signing of the Concordat, an agreement between Napoleon Bonaparte and Pope Pius VII, did not improve the situation. Though the arrangement formally recognized the Catholic Church as the nation's majority church, it did little to restore the Church and its music to their former glories, as it did not include provisions for the return of land and property that had been seized during the Revolution.[9]

When Napoleon ordered the reopening of the Chapelle royale (Tuileries Chapel) in 1802, the composition of sacred works fell back under the purview of the state. Napoleon's well-documented penchant for Italian musical styles led him to appoint Giovanni Paisiello as the director. His tenure was short; he was succeeded by Jean-François Lesueur two years later. With Lesueur and, later, Luigi Cherubini, who became his co-director, came a new aesthetic direction for French sacred music. Lesueur, along with contemporaries including Étienne-Nicolas Méhul, expanded the genre of the large-scale Revolutionary hymn—now a commonplace at the Tuileries Chapel—by exploiting the colossal performance forces that were readily at their disposal. Méhul's *Le chant national du 14 juillet 1800*, for example, utilized three orchestras, each of which accompanied separate choirs that were stationed in several spaces in the Invalides chapel. Lesueur went further; his *Le chant du 1er Vendémaire* used four orchestras and choirs, two of which were conducted by different conductors. These types of works, generally performed outdoors, brought the compositional disposition of the Revolutionary hymn from the street into the nave and set in motion an aesthetic shift upon which Berlioz would soon capitalize.[10]

Lesueur had already set this shift in motion. He was well aware of the growing disinterest in the grand motet and was working to modernize sacred works. But the unchanging nature of liturgical texts offered little room for musical invention. By supplementing the standard liturgy with additional Latin texts, he altered its meanings; by strategically distributing the newly created texts across singers and choral groups, he created narrative "scenes" that, at least in his view, might reinvigorate musical appeal and revitalize congregational interest. Lesueur's modernizations, though appreciated by the public, were not always popular with the critics and were praised even less by the clergy. He was dismissed from Notre-Dame in 1787 after only one year. Lesueur remained at the helm of the Tuileries Chapel through the Bourbon Restoration, but the chapel closed permanently in 1830. If the Revolutionary closure of *maîtrises* had gravely injured the composition of sacred music, Louis-Philippe's closure of the Tuileries Chapel sounded the death knell. Sacred music was left, for Berlioz, in a "barbarous state." At the Chapelle royale, sacred music had a purpose. Its closure meant that there was no longer an incentive for composers to write it or for teachers to teach it, given that performance opportunities were largely dictated by the liturgical year and there was thus great sensitivity to the act of experiencing such music in an appropriate setting at an appropriate time.[11]

There was, however, one last hope for Berlioz, and his name was Alexandre-Étienne Choron. He was no stranger to the world of French sacred music. Choron had established a name for himself as an editor and publisher of sacred music during the Empire, and his various essays on plainchant and sacred music led to his nomination for the task of reorganizing music in cathedrals and the royal chapel during and after the Restoration. He established his École primaire du chant in 1817; from 1820, it was known as the École royale et spéciale, and from 1825, as the Institution Royale de musique religieuse. Its early charge was to train singers for the royal chapel and as chorus musicians for the nation's theaters. Later, as the institution's mission (and name) changed, Choron's mandate was made clearer: his school was to dedicate itself to the training of church musicians and the performance of sacred music. In Choron's view, France was the only European country "without its church music," and he blamed this pathological malady on two primary causes: the predominance of plainchant in French churches and the encroachment of opera and other secular genres into any music for the church that was performed alongside of or in place of plainchant. He was dissatisfied with the fact that, as he saw it, modern performances of plainchant were more boring than edifying for the congregational listener. And though he was equally frustrated with the increasing prominence of "dramatic" music in the church, he was able to acknowledge that its presence in liturgical or paraliturgical contexts was reasonable given the fact that composing music for the stage offered French composers the most viable option for critical and financial success—when it came to sacred musical works, given the dearth of lucrative opportunity and the lack of variety within the genre, composers had little choice but to write for the stage. Should their skills be called upon in a sacred setting, Choron wrote, they often fell back upon their training, and either melded so-called theatrical compositional styles into their sacred music or imported arias or other such works wholesale into the musical fabric of the liturgy—recall Berlioz's vivid memories of hearing strains from Dalayrac's *Nina* as he took his first communion.[12]

Choron and his supporters found the sacred repertory of the sixteenth-, seventeenth-, and early eighteenth-century Italian schools to be the ideal pedagogical tool for the education of young singers. It was so effective that many preferred Choron's curriculum to that of Choron's most direct competition, the Paris Conservatoire. The "insurmountable boundary" between the Conservatoire (where singers would learn and perform secular music) and Choron's institute (where singers learned how to have careers as church musicians) was such that some critics went so far as to claim that it was Choron and Choron alone whose teaching and performances of sacred repertories could rescue French sacred music from its state of dysfunction. The prominent critic Castil-Blaze (François-Henri-Joseph Blaze) wrote that the Conservatoire's training could not possibly restore the system of *maîtrises* to their former state; Berlioz's praise for Choron was equally effusive: "Choron was not a spectator, he was an *artist* in the strongest sense of the word," he wrote, and Choron's school and the education that it offered was equivalent to the "conservation of musical art"—and all of this in a review of a concert that had nothing whatsoever to do with either Choron or his school.[13] The public, too, benefited from Choron's pedagogical work. In 1824, an agreement was made between Choron and the chapel at the Sorbonne that Choron's singers would sing Mass every Sunday. This symbiotic relationship proved useful in two ways: on the one hand, Choron's students gained practical experience putting their skills to good use while, on the other, Choron was able to quietly publicize and orient the public's taste toward his goal of revitalizing French sacred music.[14]

Despite its success and widespread popularity, the government's financial support of the institution ended with the same budgetary pruning that closed the doors of the Tuileries Chapel. From 1830 until Choron's death in 1834, the school stumbled on, damaged but not yet dead. But if the closure of choir schools had, for Berlioz, inflicted a mortal wound on the production and performance of sacred music, the potential shuttering of Choron's institute would be an even more acute blow. Berlioz implored the minister of the interior, Adolphe Thiers, not to close the institution:

Let us hope that the minister will see what an enormous gap the closing of the school for religious music would leave in musical education and that this this branch of the Conservatoire will be preserved. Let us also hope that Choron's successor will not veer away from the difficult but successful course laid out by M. Choron for, in truth, if this institution were ever to become one more cavatina factory or shop for musical cream puffs like so many others, it would be a thousand times better that it be demolished![15]

Shortly after Choron's funeral, Berlioz penned a provocative statement in the *Revue et Gazette musicale de Paris*, claiming that in the modern era, "sacred music was a rare thing." "This beautiful branch of art," Berlioz wrote, "is withering every day and will truly end up disappearing completely."[16] Berlioz's words are striking. On the one hand, his words might not seem out of place. Choron was dead, after all, and Berlioz's words eulogized the state of sacred music composition as much as they did Choron himself. On the other hand, Berlioz's obvious misgivings about the future of sacred music is curious, given his growing ambivalence toward the Church, its doctrine, and its roles in the fraught political environment of the Restoration and the Second Empire. Choron's eulogy was not the first forum in which Berlioz had written about sacred music, and it would not be the last. He took a two-pronged approach to the question of sacred music that was as equally indebted to the genre's past as it was to the continuation and strengthening of its future legacy: (1) if sacred music and religious art had the potential to be sublime, then modern music could and should be used to endow biblical or liturgical texts with their full expressive power; and (2) the scale of sacred works and the size of the forces utilized to perform them must be commensurate with the sacred spaces in question (we'll return to this point in Chapter 4). Berlioz was keenly aware of the hole that Choron's death left in an already deteriorating field of composition, and while he may not have left any single document that explains his own aesthetic understanding of sacred music, his frequent commentary on the subject—and indeed, the *Requiem* itself—is explanation enough.

SACRED MUSIC'S EXPRESSIVE POTENTIAL

Berlioz took those musicians, composers, and critics to task who stated a fundamental difference in style between sacred and secular (read: modern or "dramatic") music. Five years before Choron's death, he declared that "if the expression of feeling is the aim of one, it is also the aim of the other . . . the style of a well-conceived religious opera [*drame lyrique*] is absolutely the same as that of an oratorio. The scores of [Lesueur's *La mort d'*] *Adam* and [Rodolphe Kreutzer's] *La Mort d'Abel* are proof of it."[17] In Berlioz's opinion, the idea that liturgical music written on liturgical texts should not elicit an emotional response in the context of worship was a "strange paradox." Like Choron, he supported the belief that music's function in the church was to elevate feelings of devotion and piety through emotional responses. Why, he asked, should emotion equal impropriety?—a question that he no doubt learned to ask from Lesueur, who also believed that since the essence of modern music was dramatic, sacred music need not be deprived of modern resources. Lesueur's legacy looms large in Berlioz's view, for it was Lesueur who had established the tradition of a musical style that was fully religious but unbound by liturgical constraint through his practice of inserting biblical but non-liturgical texts into various mass settings and eliminating other traditionally required texts from others.[18] The process of setting liturgical texts themselves was paradoxical for Berlioz. At times he viewed them as overly dogmatic and responded to them with little more than indifference. In 1824, for example, he recalled feeling cold and unmoved after reading the texts of the Kyrie and the Credo.[19] At other times, however, sacred texts could be sublime. "How would," Berlioz asked, "the good performance of a fine sacred hymn offend propriety if it led to tears?" This sort of expressive sacred music could and should elicit paradoxical but not mutually exclusive responses in the listener, responses at once passionate and reverent, vehement and timidly respectful, for the expressive musical depiction of "divine love" should attain the "highest degree of religious sentiment."[20]

Berlioz's preoccupation with sacred music's expressive and affective potential stood in opposition to the stylistically and compositionally prescriptive parameters that shaped contemporaneous debates as to how French sacred music should be composed. Numerous composers and critics such as d'Ortigue, Félix Danjou, and, later, Félix Clément proclaimed plainchant as the genre par excellence of sacred music. Its appeal, according to d'Ortigue, was found in its simplicity and ease of communal performance—relative, of course, to the Renaissance polyphony that was witnessing a simultaneous growth in popularity within Parisian churches and to more modern examples of sacred music.

Moreover, d'Ortigue cast plainchant, in its resistance to secularization, as mirroring the divine qualities of permanence and eternity. D'Ortigue's contemporaries echoed his position: Félix Danjou, the organist at Notre-Dame-des-Blancs-Manteaux, Saint-Eustache, and Notre-Dame de Paris, asserted that polyphony was complicated and inaccessible to the untrained singer and concluded that polyphonic music was thus entirely unsuitable for liturgical use.[21]

Though Berlioz was not a proponent of the use of plainchant in churches to the exclusion of all else, as were many of his friends and colleagues, he also did not support the indiscriminate use of modern techniques in sacred works. The realms of the sacred and of emotional expression were not mutually exclusive, to be sure, but their interrelationships no longer squared with his youthfully innocent pleasure at hearing Dalayrac while celebrating communion. While his rhapsodic account of hearing an excerpt from a comic opera once elicited a positive emotional response—it was, after all, his earliest memory of a musical experience—he later took up Choron's view that excerpts from modern operas, set as they were with religious texts, were not appropriate for sacred use. There was only one church in Paris whose music was worthy of Berlioz's praise: Saint-Eustache. He commended the care with which the music there had been selected and performed, even when the choir had been allowed to sprinkle a bit of "musical luxury" into the worship service. Such attention to matters of appropriateness stood in opposition to the boundless liberties taken at other parishes: at Saint-Eustache, "these admirable productions have not at all been outrageously profaned by the proximity to or mixture of pieces from comic operas and solos from valve-trumpets." The music at Saint-Eustache signaled the beginning of a "reform worthy of all encouragement from friends of art."[22]

Berlioz was particularly outspoken against any sacred music that was expressive simply for the sake of effect. Liturgical texts, as bland as they may have been at times for Berlioz, should not be rendered expressive by means of arbitrary technique. Pieces of this sort were "nightmares," and those who appreciated them were worse: they were "supernightmares." Berlioz's thoughts on the matter were highlighted further in a fictionalized exchange in *Les Soirées de l'orchestre* (Evenings with the Orchestra) in which two characters discussed the setting of a text from the O Salutaris ("da robur, fer auxilium") to an "energetic phrase symbolic of strength (robur)." The rub, for Berlioz's character, was not the use of an energetic (dramatic) musical style. Rather, it was the use of a sonic marker of strength—text painting—without the slightest consideration of the text's complete meaning. Arbitrarily depicting strength *cum* sound was, in this case, empty effect and neither effective nor appropriate expression: the O Salutaris is a prayer, a supplication—a request for strength—and here, its hypothetical composer spoke in "accents far more suggestive of a threat than a supplication." This was a perfect example of what Berlioz's characters colorfully described as the "stupid style."

Berlioz thought that this sort of thoughtless effect led directly to the preference for plainchant in Parisian churches. The errant abuse of liturgical texts pushed more conservative tastes toward the belief in plainchant's musical superiority:

> Compositions in which sacred texts are treated in the would-be expressive style are overrun with similar nonsense. It is this nonsense, undoubtedly, that has given pretext for the founding of a delightful proposition on the agenda. According to this innocent heresy, the object is to preserve a truly Catholic music; actually, it tends to the total suppression of music in the divine service.... They conclude next that melody, rhythm, and modern tonality are damnable. The moderates will still accept Palestrina, but the perfervid ones, the Balfours of Burleigh of this new Puritanism, will have nothing but plainsong, raw.

This character (Macbriar, as Berlioz named him) decried modern music in the church precisely for its ability to move the emotions. The text facetiously details a scenario in which Macbriar was moved in rapturous transport after hearing the church organist inadvertently depress a single note on the keyboard: "Wonderful! Sublime! There is your genuinely religious music! That is pure art in its divine simplicity! All the rest is shamelessly profane!" "The accursed modern tonality, which is dramatic, passionate, and expressive," he continued, "should be entirely prohibited."[23] Such was a position that, in Berlioz's opinion, would be maintained at the expense of music itself.[24]

A BERLIOZIAN "AESTHETIC?"

Berlioz disliked the word "aesthetics" and generally avoided it in his criticism, correspondence, and other published writings. Though he may have claimed a general lack of adherence to broad philosophical systems or aesthetic ideologies, the level of care with which he undertook the process of defining the sounds, purposes, and effects of sacred music and the fervor with which he argued for its revitalization helps us define a Berliozian aesthetic of sacred music for ourselves. Indeed, his own words on the matter aptly introduce the possibility of an aesthetic that the *Requiem* itself confirms.[25] Debates over the suitability of so-called modern music for liturgical or otherwise sacred services were, of course, not original to the invented Macbriar, to Berlioz, or to France itself. Given the predominance of the Church in French political maneuverings and the nation's not-so-distant revolutionary past, however, these debates centered on a musical form that had the potential to affect the nation, regardless of whether its individual citizens were practicing Catholics. The Revolution had taken a great toll on the practice of Catholicism, and it exerted a similarly significant influence over sacred music. Though it catalyzed what musicians such as Choron and Berlioz saw as the near-total destruction of sacred music, the Revolution, largely through the work of composers like Lesueur, also infused the genre with a new and modern sound. Lesueur's restructuring of liturgical texts and his use of large-scale orchestral ensembles in the church created a legacy, passed on to Berlioz, that both shaped and was shaped by the musical soundscape of the Revolution.[26] But though the Revolutionary years have long been associated with a widespread secularization, or at least a deep-seated anticlerical sentiment, the Revolution did not constitute a clean break with Catholicism. Revolutionaries and Enlightenment thinkers were not reacting against religion itself. Instead, their disenchantment stemmed from a growing distaste for the Church as an institution and the persistence of religion's outward signs in everyday life.[27] Berlioz's well-documented indifference to the Church as an institution might well be a byproduct of this Revolutionary legacy; his vested interest in creating an aesthetic of sacred music, coupled with his skepticism toward institutionalized religion situates him well within this context. Berlioz was no revolutionary and though he supported the July Monarchy and Napoléon III's government, he did not share their ultra-Catholic convictions. In the aftermath of the Revolution, when Catholic practice was being actively redefined and sacred music and its institutions found themselves in a state of upheaval, Berlioz's aesthetics of sacred sound formed a sense of musical continuity that institutionalized musical life could not. He often questioned the dogmatic praxis of the Church, to be sure, but he never abandoned the Church's affective potential. That affective potential originated in no small measure from the dramatic rituals of the Catholic Church's sacraments. Perhaps it was for this reason that Berlioz consistently advocated for the dramatic potential of sacred music: much as the celebration of the Eucharist or the glowing incense that characterized the celebration of the Mass, sacred music could be both expressive *and* effective.

Berlioz's lack of interest in doctrinal praxis and his insistence that expression did not negate the sacred nature of the work at hand may well be read as embodying modern understandings of Romanticism. His views of clerically defined spirituality as rigidly prescriptive and ideologically narrow align well with the Romantic redefinition of religion and spirituality as internal, incommunicable experiences rather than communal events bound by doctrine and praxis. We might plausibly even argue that Berlioz's aesthetic of sacred music aligns more closely with a Romantic brand of secular art-religion than with any notion of the sacred itself. But though a preference for emotional expression and its attendant penchant for dramatic effect permeated Berlioz's aesthetic of sacred music, it did not solely define it. For Berlioz, expression was not the end goal. The process of crafting a truly expressive sacred music went well beyond the *Requiem*'s reconfigured texts, large-scale orchestrations, and frequently colossal performance forces. Such binary distinctions between devotion and drama, or expression and sincerity, obscured the true purpose of Berlioz's aesthetic of sacred music: to move the listener to a state of, as he described it at his first communion, "a kind of mystical, passionate unrest"—in short, the sublime. Berlioz's vocal participation in the debates over sacred music and its musical byproducts were anchored in his understanding and experience of the sacred sublime. In the *Requiem*, then, Berlioz exploited his aesthetic views to their fullest potential by crafting a sonic experience that was equal parts sacred and sublime.

CHAPTER 3

EXPERIENCING
THE REQUIEM

BERLIOZ AND THE
SACRED SUBLIME

[Berlioz] wanted to paint sublime horrors and the terrors of the last judgment. The heavens open, the son of God appears on the clouds, tombs shatter, and as the heavenly trumpets' agonizing voice resounds from the four corners of the earth, the dead are raised and appear before the Lord while shaking dust off their bones. The composer rendered this sublime tableau with piercing colors. Sixty trumpets and brass instruments respond to each other from the four corners of the formidable orchestra; sixteen timpani unite their funereal rumblings in this thunder, and when this mass of harmony bursts forth at once, shaking the church's vaults with its powerful waves, it is impossible to describe the impression that seized the entire audience. All heads bowed, all hearts shook with a religious terror, and they shuddered until the last note was extinguished.[1]

Berlioz's Requiem. Jennifer Walker, Oxford University Press. © Oxford University Press 2025.
DOI: 10.1093/9780197688847.003.0004

Musically painting sublime horrors, as this critic highlighted with such rhetorical flourish, was a unique achievement of Berlioz's *Requiem*, a genre that had its fill of sonic evocations of the last judgment from Mozart to Cherubini. But what does this concept—one that is notoriously difficult to define—represent for the composer and his audience? There is no single experience of the sublime, nor can it be distilled into hard-and-fast descriptive (or prescriptive) taxonomies. Is the sublime a rhetorical ideal, attained through a certain grandeur of thought, the evocation of vivid passions, and the effective use of figures of speech, elevated diction, and harmonious literary structures? Is the sublime a feeling, a sense of elevation, of transport, brought on by the sight of a mountain or the experience of an earthquake? Is the sublime an attribute of the mind or of the natural world and its phenomena? Can we, like the critic described above, hear "the sublime"?

Historically speaking, the sublime has encompassed all the above. Theories of the sublime, ranging from Longinus to Edmund Burke to Immanuel Kant, have generally outlined the sublime as a descriptor for the immeasurable and incomprehensible grandeur of sites, thoughts, places, and experiences. The Longinian sublime was largely rhetorical and originated from the terrifying and awe-inspiring experience of the natural world, whether oceans, mountains, thunder, or earthquakes. Burke's writings on the subject and Kant's third critique shifted the perspective to the Enlightenment subject. They understood the sublime as an experience through which the thinking, rational subject was confronted with something too great for comprehension or resistance. As a result, man (the subject was masculine for these authors) underwent a painful confrontation trying to confront his awe and then overcame the pain in a moment of release or self-realization. Experiencing the sublime, particularly following Burke and Kant, encompassed a three-part process: a sudden event, scene, sight, or sound incapacitates the mind through its often-terrifying force, thus interrupting the ability to act freely or to reason. This sense of terror, or overwhelm, is heightened by the subject's realization of their own inadequacy to comprehend and overcome it; the intense emotional experience is only made complete by a realization that this terror-inducing event is also one that causes pleasure or delight—indeed, for Burke, sublimity can be achieved only when the subject is faced with both fear and pleasure.

Nicolas Boileau's 1674 translation of Longinus' *Peri hypsous* (On the sublime) into French plucked the Greek treatise from relative obscurity and into the hands of literary theorists and writers who would become the early champions of what is now recognized as aesthetics. From Boileau came the separation of sublime transcendence (Longinus' *hypsous*) from sublime rhetorical styles and devices. Put another way, Boileau differentiated between the truly sublime—a critical concept—and the sublime style—a set of rhetorical devices. A telltale sign of difference between *le sublime* and *le style sublime* was simplicity, for it was in simplicity that the ethical and aesthetic dimensions of the sublime intersected: as a contrast to effect for effect's sake, simplicity—grandeur without artifice—acted as an aesthetic embodiment of the desirable values of honor and sincerity: "Be artfully simple, sublime without pride, pleasant without artifice."[2] Over the centuries, French musicians and critics in turn embraced and spurned simplicity as an emblem of the sublime.

In whichever manner one chooses to define or understand it, sublimity engages with several fundamental questions. Wrestling with the concept of the sublime also means that we must wrestle with the very idea of knowledge: how, the concept of the sublime infers, can we come to know things that are found outside the everyday, the easily understood, the mundane. The sublime also creates a complex web of power dynamics: who decides what is and what is not sublime? How should events, sights, or thoughts that trigger sublimity be handled and/or evaluated? Hearing Berlioz's *Requiem* in the nineteenth century was, for many, a sublime experience. If the experience of the sublime described above was rooted in religious terror, then Berlioz's engagement with it—or even creation of it—required his awareness of the numerous ways in which contemporary audiences understood, appreciated, and evaluated sublimity. At its core, the sublime asks us to consider the very nature of bodily and cognitive experiences, for sublimity is ultimately a sensory experience.[3]

BERLIOZ'S MUSICAL SUBLIME

When we think of the musical sublime, we must also consider it as an experience that can be crafted or curated by a human subject. If some understandings of the sublime were rooted in experiences of the natural world, unspoiled by human hands, then other conceptions of sublimity— Boileau's, for instance—relied on generative work that had to be created first in order to be experienced through the senses. The sublime was, according to Aubin-Louis Millin, an early nineteenth-century antiquary and naturalist, "the highest perfection of art" that effected "admiration, veneration, a violent desire, great courage, or else terror and fear—everywhere, in a word, where one wants to restrain or vigorously excite the activity of intellectual forces."[4] Berlioz often used the term "sublime" as the highest of accolades, but the evidence suggests that he also understood it to be an aesthetic category that was worthy of consideration as such.[5] Berlioz's understanding of experiencing musical sublimity, like Millin's, was predicated on a simultaneously aesthetic, emotional, cognitive, and sensory experience that was profound, often excessive, and genuine. He was well acquainted with Boileau's writings, having no doubt been introduced to them as a youngster by his father, and references to Boileau's ideas appeared frequently in his correspondence and criticism.[6] Things began to change, however, with the idea of an immersive and multisensory experience. Excess was no longer something to criticize, for it was in the monumental that the sublime could be understood as finding its greatest expression, and it was in the orchestral music of Beethoven that Berlioz found the most profoundly monumental sublimity. Berlioz's reviews of Beethoven's symphonies described them as mysterious, unpredictable, and powerful, and this power often elicited a response that moved beyond an elevation to sublimity into a physiological reaction that defied the mind's physical capacity for understanding. In his reflections on the sublime, Berlioz attributed such characteristics even to select instruments: the bass trombone, which features prominently alongside the flute in the *Requiem*'s Hostias, was "majestic, formidable, and awe-inspiring," and he conceived of his ideal orchestra in much the same way.[7] This sort of orchestral model not only signified the sublime, it *was* sublime:

> [It would have an] incalculable melodic, expressive, and rhythmic power, a penetrating force like no other, a prodigious sensitivity in all nuances of ensemble and detail. . . . When at rest it would be majestic like a slumbering ocean. When in a state of agitation, it would recall tropical storms. It would erupt like a volcano. It would convey the laments, whispers, and mysterious sounds of virgin forests, the shouts, prayers, songs of triumph or lamentation of a people with an expansive soul, an ardent heart, and fiery passions. Its silence would strike awe through its solemnity, and the most recalcitrant temperaments would shudder at the sight of its surging crescendo, like the roar of an immense and sublime conflagration![8]

Berlioz's ideal orchestra was large—it was, in his own words, "monumental"—and it could be evocative of images of vastness and natural power, or it could catalyze an overpowering, embodied, and physical experience of the sublime.[9] When, for example, he described the effect that hearing the Et iterum venturus from his *Messe solennelle* (1825) had upon him, he felt that he "swam on this agitated sea [and] sniffed these floods of sinister vibrations." And it was not just Berlioz who had such a reaction: when a mighty roll of the timpani signaled the dread of weeping and gnashing of teeth, "the entire church trembled."[10] This terror-filled, embodied, and neurophysical response to hearing the Et iterum venturus, however, was only magnified after increasing the size of the orchestra in a revised version of the *Messe solennelle*. Performed two years later with unison singing and an expanded orchestra of six trumpets, four horns, three trombones, and two ophicleides, the same passage, now "thunderous," induced a "convulsive tremor" and rendered Berlioz nearly unable to stand. Its effect—a sense of sublime terror depicted aurally as thunder—was only compounded by the already sublime nature of his enlarged and "noticeably improved" orchestra.[11]

It should come as no surprise that Berlioz would adopt this sublime orchestral model in the *Requiem* or other works that he identified as monumental. He did not, however, consider such compositions to be "gigantic," "colossal," or even monumentally sublime based on size and scale alone. Instead, he claimed, it was also the "breadth of style and the formidably slow and deliberate pace of certain progressions, whose final goal cannot be guessed, that give these works their peculiarly 'gigantic' character and 'colossal' aspect."[12] Such stylistic and harmonic choices were a clear marker of the sublime for Berlioz, who identified similar characteristics in his teacher Jean-François Lesueur's sacred works. Lesueur's *Premier Oratorio du Sacre* (1836), composed for the coronation of Charles X, was exemplary of his monumental style. While slow-moving harmonies that changed once per measure, an "enormous orchestral design," and a total absence of decorative ornament led some critics to criticize the work as heavy, boring, and monotonous, Berlioz praised it as majestic and imposing.[13] He replicated these techniques in his own *Requiem*, fully understanding that the inability to predict any given progression's next harmonic move could lead an attentive listener into a state of sublimity (Example 3.1). The "consequence of such vastness of scale," he explained, is that a listener "either misses the point altogether or is overwhelmed by a tremendous emotion. Often at performances of my

EXAMPLE 3.1A: Hector Berlioz, Hostias, *Requiem*, mm. 1–12. Transcribed from *NBE 9* (1978).

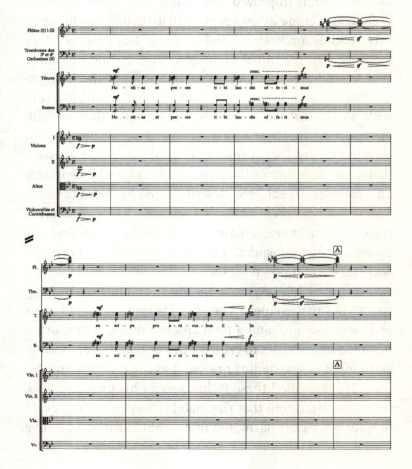

EXAMPLE 3.1B: Hector Berlioz, Agnus Dei, *Requiem*, mm. 1–13. Transcribed from *NBE 9* (1978).

Requiem, one man will be trembling, shaken to the depths of his soul, while the man next to him sits there listening intently and understanding nothing."[14]

Monumentality and "sonorous overkill" were not the only factors for Berlioz in determining whether a musical work was sublime. If scale was a clear sonic marker of the sublime, so too was its opposite: a deliberate and meticulous attention to minute detail that resulted in a focused yet similar experience of the unforeseeable unknown by the listener. Berlioz was well aware of the Janus-faced nature of sublimity: for every movement in the *Requiem* that utilizes the full battery of supplementary brass and percussion, the movement immediately following is noticeably smaller-scale and more devotional in nature. Sandwiched in between the Tuba mirum and the Rex tremendae, the Quid sum miser features unison singing scored with only English horn, bassoon, and strings. The Quaerens me, an a cappella paean to imitative counterpoint, forms a contrast that highlights the dualities inherent in Berlioz's understanding of the sublime with the Rex tremendae and the Lacrymosa. Sublimity was also referential. According to Longinus, the invocation of past sublime creators resulted in a new sublime work of art in itself: it was, in essence, a technique of imitation in which past evocations of sublimity were claimed as models for a new, current sublimity.[15] For Berlioz, Lesueur was sublime, and the closeness with which Berlioz modeled Lesueur's sublimity as he formulated his own aesthetic understanding of sacred music might well be described as the invocation of one sublime in the creation of another. Indeed, Berlioz's own reworkings of his earlier and self-described sublime *Messe solennelle* in the *Requiem*—the opening of the *Requiem*'s Tuba mirum appeared first as the Resurrexit in the *Messe solennelle*— may also be read as a mechanism for producing a newly sublime work, as could the claims that the speed with which Berlioz completed the composition of the *Requiem* was possible in part by his incorporation of previously written (or at least sketched) musical ideas.[16] Berlioz's approach to sublimity, then, was particularly syncretic. If, for Longinus, an author's (or composer's) ability to fashion deeply intricate conceptions or ideas was a quality that allowed the effective communication of a subject's inherent sublimity and, for Kant, sublimity was both dynamical (based in terror and fright) and mathematical (expansive, deliberate, complex), then Berlioz's manipulations of his ideal orchestra and his frequent recall of differing and past sublimities in the *Requiem* heightened the work's sublimity and the listening subject's ability to experience it as such.

HEARING THE SACRED SUBLIME

If the aesthetic experience of sublimity was not a wholly sacred experience per se, it was nonetheless substantively intertwined with Western religion as writers like Burke and Kant and composers like Berlioz understood it. The sacred, the sonic, and the sublime shared numerous points of intersection, even in an age during which a philosophical and aesthetic concept of art-religion was favored over institutionalized religion. Boileau had already fashioned a connection between the sacred and the sublime: his translation of Longinus highlighted the famous *fiat lux* ("Let there be light") passage as a prime example of sublimity. It provided the perfect contrast between the sublime and the sublime style. "Let there be light, and there was light" (Genesis 1:3) was powerfully sublime in its connection of sublimity with religious transcendence. Lacking grandiose workings of syntax and language, it was sublime in its simplicity, and it also strategically suggested that the sublime straddled the divide between the sacred (the Bible) and the secular (rhetoric).[17]

In the nineteenth century, the concept of the sublime offered, furthermore, a highly attractive means of absorbing religious practice into an artistic one, with concerts providing a communal yet more secularized experience of transcendence. The ideas that transferred Boileau's model of a sacred sublime related to contemporaneous French religious practice and their homilies that relied on the fundamental relationship between the speaker (or priest) and the subject being treated. Was the speaker an impassioned orator whose well-formed words and thoughts could create a sublime experience, or was the speaker a passive vessel through which the sacred sublime flowed, already formed by the innate sublimity of the sacred subject at hand? Well before Berlioz's time, the bishop Jacques-Bénigne Bossuet wrote the following about the art of preaching in a sublime style:

> Preachers who greatly animate their voice, their gestures, all of their actions, who speak with a loud and firm tone, who appear impassioned and steeped in the truths that they teach, despite saying only common things, without any of the artifice of eloquence, touch their Listeners much more easily than eloquent Preachers who dryly and coldly give polished sermons about higher truths. . . . There are those who set about preaching in the grand style with a subtlety of thought, a justness of phrasing, an abundance of polished and inflated expressions. All these things can form a sublime style, but are not grand, as we understand it.[18]

Bossuet's "sublime style" was grounded in pathos and expression, the grand style in adherence to convention and measured affect. Like Boileau, he posited a difference between the truly sublime and a superficially sublime style (the beautiful); Berlioz was as familiar with Bossuet's idea of the grand style as he was with Boileau's body of work.[19] The relationship between sacred texts, the vocal delivery of the sermon, and the congregation's response to it was paramount in Bossuet's description. Preachers reflected on the efficacy of their words, delivered aurally as the homily, through their successful elevation of their listeners to a religiously sublime state. The power of the liturgy and of the homily for the faithful was found in its ability to achieve results—conversions or elevations—and thus the sacred sublime moved beyond the Longinian brand of sublimity as effect (shock, awe, terror, etc.). And if, for Longinus, the sublime was cast as primarily discursive in nature, for later theorists such as Boileau, the experience of the sublime was closely related with sound. Take the *fiat lux*, for example: the sublime sound of God's voice commanding light was heard, and it was made so. Theologians thus afforded a special importance to sensory perception: God's voice was often likened to thunder and other natural sounds—literally, metaphorically, and through aural delivery—while the voice of Christ was given sonic attributes of sweetness, humility, and humanity. Each was an aspect of the sacred sublime, for as Burke and others formulated it, just as monumentality was a marker of the sublime, so too was the "last extreme of littleness": if God's voice was to be translated as thunderous booming through a pastor's "greatly animated" voice, Christ's voice required a nearly silent attentiveness to be heard.[20] The sacred sublime, then, was a sublimity that was best experienced by hearing and listening.

THE REQUIEM *AND THE SACRED SUBLIME(S)*

Notwithstanding his frustration with the current state of the genre, Berlioz appreciated the potential sublimity of sacred musical works and the biblical or liturgical texts on which they were based. If he was largely unmoved by the doctrinal aspects of the Church, he was still convinced that sacred music, when not beholden to constricting formulae and dull aesthetic conventions, should be and was sublime. Religious texts were "sublime subjects"; religious music that was properly expressive of religious thought could lead to a potentially sublime experience.[21] The critic Joseph d'Ortigue and Berlioz fought over many things, but they agreed on the fact that sacred music was sublime as and for itself and that it could and should elevate the listener into a sublime state. But whereas d'Ortigue and his likeminded colleagues held that plainchant most closely resembled an ideal of the sacred sublime—unchanging, timeless, and pure—Berlioz took a more Longinian approach to the idea and followed on Bossuet's affective heels. Like sublimely terrifying natural phenomena or the impassioned sublimity of Bossuet's ideal manner of preaching, Berlioz's approach to sonic sacred sublimity was one predicated on the "sternly majestic ideas" that the sublime subject had to offer. As Berlioz understood it, the power of sacred music for the listener was found in its ability to elevate the listener to the sublime, provided that the effect—perhaps even the sublime style—was not simply intended to titillate the senses: the goal of sacred music was to "move and elevate the soul by expressing the feelings that infuse the words to which it was set."[22] The inherent drama that Berlioz saw in sacred music—the mystical terror and passionate unrest that characterized the musical landscape of Berlioz's first communion and his body's physiologically sublime responses to his hearing of the *Messe solennelle*—was as much about his aesthetic understanding of what the genre required for survival as it was about moving the listener to a state of sublimity that made the synthesis of the expressive and the ecclesiastical not only possible, but desirable.

The *Requiem* draws on numerous modes of sublimity as an aesthetic category, all of which coalesced into a musical experience that registered as truly sublime for numerous critics. It would be quite simple to connect the *Requiem* to the sublime on a surface level; the sheer size of the orchestra and choir at certain times suffices to make the point. Musically speaking, sublimity often cultivates a seeming transgression in terms of size; we have come to expect that works identified as sublime have, in some way, breached the acceptable limits of orchestral or choral convention. Given its potential for an all-enveloping acoustic effect, music was able to offer a more dramatic and more physically engaged experience, much unlike the other arts at the time—the bigger, the better. Yet even if their reviews often betrayed a somewhat simplistic connection between monumentality and sublimity, critics of the various performances of the *Requiem* in the first half of the nineteenth century rarely identified the work as a sonic transgression. If Berlioz's penchant for monumental orchestration—the Dies irae's four supplemental brass ensembles, for example—appeared frequently in reviews, it was done so more in the service of connecting the experience of hearing such forces with the sublime than criticizing it for any perceived theatricality. The Dies irae, identified by one unnamed critic as "the pitfall of all Requiem masses that have been set to music," was no stumbling block for Berlioz. It was instead a "terrifying concept," and the Tuba mirum was undoubtedly "one of the most frightening and most alarming effects that music has attempted." Berlioz had rendered the cries of the souls in Purgatory audible in his "sublime musical conception," and all the markers of the sacred sublime were present: terrors for the guilty, delights for the elect, groans, prayers, and convulsions.[23] At the sound of the Tuba mirum, "an electric shiver ran among the twenty thousand listeners that filled the church: all rose involuntarily [with] fright and admiration painted on their faces."[24] And though the *Requiem* was described by the critic Ernest Dubreuil as a "colossus of harmony" and a "marvel of instrumentation," it was not the product of any desire for drama or simple effect. Performers and audience members alike held back tears as they heard the musical depiction of the sublime terror of the souls in Purgatory; they were "terrified with emotion."[25] For these writers, the Tuba mirum embodied multiple modes of sublimity: it combined terror with pleasure—an emotional experience of sublimity that catalyzed a collective physiological response marked by electric shivers and involuntary movements. Even the church itself was unable to escape the sublime terror that filled the space. Anthropomorphized vaults likewise trembled under the terror-filled and thunderous sounding of the final trumpet.[26]

But the sincerity of the sublime experience described by many writers upon hearing the Tuba mirum came as a pleasant surprise to others who had become accustomed to hearing Berlioz's idiosyncratic writing as the product of his purported love for theatrical effect. Knowing the substantial role that the brass would play in the *Requiem*, a writer in 1837 worried that the result would be noisy simply for the sake of showmanship. One doubting critic wholeheartedly embraced the composer's monumental sounds: "This time again we had to worry for the Requiem Mass because we knew that the brass had a huge part in the performance.... However, it was not so.... The wholly dreaded brass and kettledrums were reserved almost exclusively for the Dies irae, but this time, Berlioz used them with all energy and effect not to produce a vain noise, but to spread a sublime terror on all his audience."[27] Another critic related the experience of hearing the *Requiem* as going beyond one of listening to acoustic oddities composed only for shock value into one that moved the audience into a sublime experience of emotional transport:

> Are these processes of instrumentation, perfected or invented by Berlioz, only curiosities of acoustics? Do they stop at our ears, or do they make us shudder with enthusiasm and dread, quiver with joy and hope? Here is the entire question. In this scene of the last judgment, is it only noise that you hear? Does it not seem to you that the bowels of the earth are tearing themselves apart, that the world dissolves, and does this convulsive agony of nature say nothing to your imagination?[28]

And whereas settings of the Requiem Mass by Mozart and Cherubini already boasted considerable reputations, they were, according to Berlioz's contemporary, the composer Léon Kreutzer, regrettably inspired by an overwhelming aura of sadness and sorrow rather than "energy" and "terror." By contrast, he found Berlioz's work completely immersed in a wave of majesty and terror—each was a constituent part of a sublime experience on its own but, taken together, they became the pinnacle of the simultaneously awe-inspiring and terrifying sublime experience. Hearing the cries of the departed, the thunder of the last trumpet, the dissolving of the earth into apocalyptic ash: such was an encounter of sublimity that moved beyond sheer effect and orchestral noise (*le style sublime*) into true sublimity (*le sublime*) without exceeding the acceptable limits of good taste.[29]

The idea of judgment, divine retribution, and the afterlife as anguished torment is one that has permeated Christian theology for centuries, but it was a veritable obsession in late eighteenth- and early nineteenth-century France. Berlioz himself had an abiding interest in these ideas, having considered recycling elements of the *Messe solennelle* in an oratorio on the subject in the early 1830s (the incomplete and now lost *Le Dernier Jour du monde*). Even the critical reception of the Dies irae as sublime fell nicely in step with the theology and styles of preaching in France at the time. Religious conversions—the experience of the sacred sublime par excellence—were affected not only by sublime modes of homiletic delivery, but also through the content of such sublime orations. Catholic doctrine then was predicated on fear and retribution rather than love and forgiveness; the Church was likewise seen to be uncompromisingly punitive. The French sacred sublime was terror at its greatest—gone were the Burkean notions of pleasurable relief—yet it simultaneously embraced and moved beyond the Longinian sublime: though it was deeply dependent on shock, wonder, and awe to be effective, the sacred sublime was focused on achieving measurable results. Hearing the *Requiem*, then, was much like hearing a French Catholic sermon in the early nineteenth century: access to the sacred sublime was always given by an intermediary (a preacher or, in this case, the composer and his performers). Its impassioned modes of delivery sought to strike terror in the hearts of its audience, a corollary to the hellfire and damnation style of preaching that dominated French theology at the time. But the success of the sacred sublime was as much about its reception as such as it was the methods of its production: did the hearing subject perceive the aural event as sublime, and did the process render the experience appropriately religious? For Joseph Mainzer, Berlioz had failed. In his effort to create music that represented "judgment itself, the destruction of worlds, the resurrection of the departed, and all the devilry of Dante's hell," Berlioz failed to depict the pious believer's *feelings* about the final judgment.[30] Mainzer's grievances against Berlioz notwithstanding, it was precisely this musical depiction of judgment that rendered the experience sublime for other writers, for Berlioz had gone beyond the superficial nature of feelings into the transformative nature of sublimity. The *Requiem* was, in fact, so successful at embodying the sacred sublime that it had the potential to effect conversions, and Berlioz stood in as Boileau and Bossuet's impassioned pastor: "this music was a true sermon," wrote the critic Alphonse de Calonne, and its purpose was "fulfilled so energetically that one would not be surprised to learn that Berlioz caused several conversions on that day."[31]

If Berlioz's nineteenth-century listeners heard the *Requiem* as an eschatologically sublime sermon, then the text and the text's musical mediators must also be considered as agents of the sublime experience. The processes of developing and understanding faith in the Catholic tradition was first and foremost an aural one that was created through the clergy's mediation of sacred texts. Outside the home, where devotional literature might lead to quiet contemplation, access to the holy texts and their meaning was always given by an intermediary through verbal, aural delivery. The legitimacy and agency of the speaker, then, and that speaker's shaping of scripture and of divine words, were of utmost importance, for a successful delivery enabled the listener's transport to sacred sublimity. Berlioz appreciated what he perceived to be not only the potentially sublime nature of sacred texts and religious subjects but also the power that their traditional aurality could carry. As he shaped the liturgical text in his setting of the *Requiem*, Berlioz highlighted and reconfigured those sections that he understood to be the most sublime in the context of contemporaneous French theology and current discourses on the sublime. He accentuated the theological and homiletic contrast between eschatological judgment (God's voice as an agent of retribution) and redemptive salvation (Jesus as savior) through a combination of textual adaptation and stylistic contrast. After the sublime clangor of the Tuba mirum, the Quid sum miser enters with, as Berlioz notated it, "a feeling of humility and fear." Its introductory measures, pared down to two English horns, two bassoons, cellos, and basses, simultaneously recall two motives from the Dies irae: while the English horns and, later, the tenors, reprise the soprano's opening salvo, the bassoons and strings repeat the Dies irae's plainchant-inspired melodic introduction, all in an effort to foreground the same sense of sublime terror that had been so prominently heard in the Dies irae (Example 3.2). From the tumult of the ever-building textures and the sounds of trembling and the final trumpets of the Dies irae, the majority of which are based on the same two melodic motives, emerge the tenors, who sing the same plaintive motive in unison. The narrative observation of eschatological terror, made from a third-person perspective in the Dies irae, gives way to prayers of awestruck supplication spoken by the departed soul in the first person. "What shall *I*, a wretch, say then," asks the speaker. "To which protector shall *I* appeal?," he implores, when even the righteous is hardly safe. As the seventh stanza in the Dies irae, the question posed by the speaker in the Quid sum miser would traditionally be followed by the answer given in the next stanza (Rex tremendae, "King of awful majesty"). Berlioz's setting of the Quid sum miser, however, combines stanzas seven, nine, and seventeen; stanza eight is heard as the beginning of the next movement (see Example 3.3).

EXAMPLE 3.2: Hector Berlioz, Quid sum miser, *Requiem*, mm. 1–12. Transcribed from *NBE 9* (1978).

EXAMPLE 3.3 Texts of the Quid sum miser

Traditional Liturgical Text	Berlioz's Reconfiguration
7. Quid sum miser tunc dicturus? quem patronum rogaturus, cum vir justus sit securus?	[7] Quid sum miser tunc dicturus? quem patronum rogaturus, cum vir justus sit securus?
8. Rex tremendae majestatis, qui salvandos salvas gratis, salva me, fons pietatis.	[9] Recordare, pie Jesu quod sum causa tuae viae ne me perdas illa die [17] oro supplex et acclinis cor contritum quasi cinis gere curam mei finis.
[What shall I, a wretch, say then? To which protector shall I appeal when even the just man is barely safe?	[What shall I, a wretch, say then? To which protector shall I appeal when even the just man is barely safe? Remember, gentle Jesus,
King of awful majesty, Thou freely savest those worthy of salvation. Save me, fount of pity.]	that I am the reason for your time on earth. Do not cast me out on that day. I pray, suppliant and kneeling, a heart as contrite as ashes. Take Thou my ending into thy care.]

If the standard liturgical text suggests that the protector in question is the terror-filled "king of awful majesty," Berlioz's textual adaptation positions Jesus—"gentle Jesus," as stanza nine suggests—as the ultimate redeemer. And if the sounds of approaching God, the divine judge, on the day of wrath first evoked a sonic model of sublime terror, the sounds of the supplicant's entreaties to Jesus' gentility bring forth a sublimity based simultaneously in French homiletics and Burkean philosophy. If greatness of dimension and impassioned speaking were markers of the sublime, so too were smallness, silence, and a character altogether different from the terrible: the difference between the monumental sublime and its minute counterpart was indistinguishable. In his smallness, the speaker, intoned by unison singing, recalls the sonic reminiscences of the terrible day of wrath and is, in the end, rendered equally sublime by virtue of the combination of his awestruck contrition, small-voiced supplication, and the reminder that sublime terror is never far away.

The traditional Rex tremendae, though displaced by Berlioz's textual patchwork, returns to the model of the monumental sublime. A fanfare-like burst from the full and supplemental orchestras shatters the quiet stillness of the Quid sum miser as God's terrible majesty becomes the speaker's focal point; dotted rhythms, performed at *forte* or above by the full battery of performers, signal the subject's royalty—his "awful majesty." Yet for as quickly as the speaker implores the divine judge for mercy, Berlioz shifts the narrative focus back to "gentle Jesus": the first-person subject's possible redemption by Jesus, heard already in the Quid sum miser, remains the primary focus of the Rex tremendae. Here again Berlioz switches between sonic modes of sublimity. If the movement's opening section evinces the king's terrible sublimity through recognizable musical topoi of royalty and monumentality, the music accompanying the textual and narrative shift ("qui salvandos salvas gratis") recalls a different yet equally potent sublimity (Example 3.4).

Berlioz's sonic emphases on the contrasts between God's retributive and Jesus's salvific voices are made even more audible through further textual revisions. The incorporation

EXAMPLE 3.4A: Hector Berlioz, Rex tremendae, *Requiem*, mm. 1–3. Transcribed from *NBE 9* (1978).

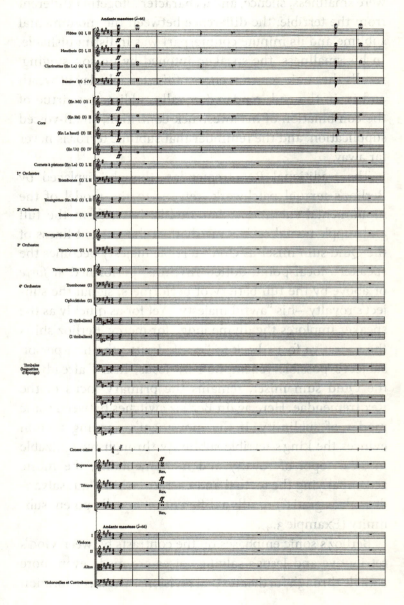

EXAMPLE 3.4B: Hector Berlioz, Rex tremendae, *Requiem*, mm. 16–19. Transcribed from *NBE 9* (1978).

of the Confutatis (stanza sixteen) into the Rex tremendae and the Recordare (stanzas eight and nine) creates an alternation between the divine voices of terror and redemption. As the speaker experiences increased fear about his final destiny, melodic sequences and a full orchestral accompaniment prepare the entrance of the Confutatis text. But the flame-ridden eternity that awaits the damned, accompanied by full and *fortissimo* brass and woodwind doubling, is suddenly interrupted by a *pianissimo* cry to Jesus (Example 3.5). Berlioz's striking addition of "Jesu" to his setting of the text, in combination with his slight grammatical alterations that retain first-person positionality, is punctuated by his use of silence. The many damned, having been reduced to

EXAMPLE 3.5: Hector Berlioz, Rex tremendae, *Requiem*, mm. 42–44. Transcribed from *NBE 9* (1978).

a single speaker through Berlioz's editorial work, beseech Jesus for divine deliverance ("voca me") and are followed immediately by a measure of silence—meticulously marked as "silence" in the score—and *sotto voce*, nearly unaccompanied singing (Example 3.6).

A drastic reduction in size, scale, and force marks the Quaerens me—the movement praised by several contemporaneous reviewers as the work's most appropriately religious movement. "Palestrinian" in nature, the brief, a cappella,

EXAMPLE 3.6: Hector Berlioz, Rex tremendae, *Requiem*, mm. 56–57. Transcribed from *NBE* 9 (1978).

and imitative movement is an exercise in pared-down sublimity.[32] Save for a brief crescendo to *sforzando* at the midpoint and a crescendo to *forte* near the end, the dynamic level never rises above *piano*. Here the speaker prays again for divine salvation from the first-person perspective prepared by the preceding movements and outlines in basic terms the foundational tenets and most sublime aspect of Christian theology: that Jesus' death was the ultimate act of salvation for worthy supplicants and that the promise of this redemption is steadfast (Example 3.7). The same processes of textual adaptation and compositional "smallness" characterize the Offertoire, particularly following the

EXAMPLE 3.7: Hector Berlioz, Quaerens me, *Requiem*, mm. 1–8. Transcribed from *NBE 9* (1978).

vastness of the Lacrymosa. The text of the Offertoire again highlights elements of salvation, yet it further emphasizes the Old Testament promises of favor and deliverance made by God to Abraham (Example 3.8).

Here the vocal line, comprising a single rhythmic unit and sung in unison throughout by sopranos, tenors, and basses, utilizes only two notes throughout (Example 3.9). The first—and only—change in the melodic line comes after 137 measures in perfect alignment with Berlioz's adapted text. From a continuous oscillation between two pitches in a minor mode comes a statement of promise, made in the parallel major and staggered between the full choir. Though

EXAMPLE 3.8: Texts of the Offertory/Offertoire

Traditional Liturgical Text

Domine Jesu Christe, Rex gloriae, libera anima cmnium fidelium defunctorum de poenis inferni et de profundo lacu.

[Lord Jesus Christ, King of glory, deliver all the faithful souls of the departed from the pains of hell and the deep pit.

Libera eas de ore leonis, ne absorbeat eas Tartarus, ne cadant in obscurum: sec signifer sanctus Michael repraesentet eas in lucem sanctam, quam olim Abrahae promisisti, et semini ejus.

Deliver them from the lion's mouth, that hell does not engulf them ror that they fall into darkness: let Saint Michael the standard-bearer lead them into the holy light that Thou promised to Abraham and his seed.]

Berlioz's Setting

Domine Jesu Christe, Rex gloriae, libera animas omnium fidelium defunctorum de poenis inferni et de profundo lacu.

[Lord Jesus Christ, King of glory, deliver all the faithful souls of the departed from the pains of hell and the deep pit.

Et sanctus Michael signifer repraesentet eas in lucem sanctam, quam olim Abrahae et semini ejus **promisisti.**

And let Saint Michael the standard-bearer lead them into the holy light that to Abraham and his seed you **promised.**

Domine Jesu Christe. Amen.

Lord Jesus Christ. Amen.]

the melodic content of this brief section is derivative of the earlier half-step motive, the textural change, when taken in combination with the textual adaptation, is striking. In a whisper (*ppp*) and with little orchestral accompaniment, the choir sings of the promise of Jesus' future redemption ("promisisti"), a promise made even more evident through Berlioz's syntactic repositioning and compositional contrast (Example 3.10).

Set in arguably the most appropriately sacred manners— that is, lacking the grandiosity that d'Ortigue and others

EXAMPLE 3.9: Hector Berlioz, Offertoire, *Requiem*, mm. 6–11. Transcribed from *NBE 9* (1978).

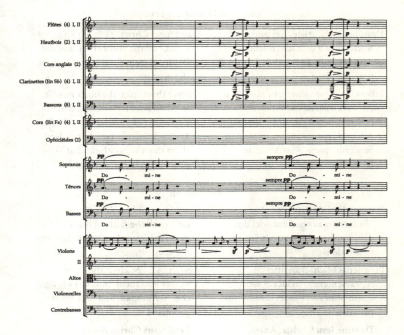

saw as modern and dramatic—the two movements that encapsulate fundamental elements of Christian theology were rendered audibly sublime through the careful rendering of contrasting divine voices: the work was, according to the composer and critic Prosper Sain d'Arod, "sublime, sublime, for a third time, sublime!"[33]

Considering the positionalities of the liturgical speaker, Berlioz's careful editing of the sacred text, and the sound of the divine in homiletic and theological practice aligns the *Requiem* with multiple modes of sublimity that extend beyond the monumental sublimity captured by contemporaneous critics. If some of his critics indicted his

EXAMPLE 3.10: Hector Berlioz, Offertoire, *Requiem*, mm. 137–42. Transcribed from *NBE 9* (1978).

extravagant orchestrations as the byproduct of an uncomfortable association with materialistic program music, his supporters recognized the same musical idiosyncrasies as having shaped a listening experience that they experienced as profoundly sublime. Berlioz's manipulations and reworkings of the Latin texts are calibrated carefully to highlight the most sublime language of the Mass for the dead, thus enabling Berlioz's most sublime musical moments to be understood as such. The sublime, for Berlioz, was predicated as much on his understanding of the aesthetics of sacred music and his belief that sacred texts are themselves sublime as it was on his much more well-known interest in medicine, physiology, and the fantastic. By ensounding those aspects of the reworked texts through means recognized as sublime in homiletic and theological discourse, Berlioz painted a musical picture of the sacred sublime that encompassed aspects of sound and orchestration that move beyond innovation, experimentation, theatricality, vastness, and monumentality. But crafting an appropriately sacred body of music for the church or a sublime *Requiem* went beyond aesthetics and compositional practice for Berlioz, for the truly sublime sacred experience was also dependent on how architectural and physical space functioned as an agent of musicality and of the sublime.

CHAPTER 4

BUILDING THE REQUIEM

BERLIOZ AS AURAL ARCHITECT

> In the Tuba mirum, I had the impression that every little column on church's pillars became a pipe and the church itself became an immense organ.[1]

While in Rome as a Prix de Rome laureate, Berlioz found sublime inspiration at Saint Peter's basilica. It was one of his first stops in the city, and he wrote of his experiences there with great fondness. It was "sublime" and "overpowering"; he recalled sights and sounds enjoyed there with vivid detail. Of obvious importance to Berlioz was the sheer grandeur of the building itself. But if the cathedral's "giant architecture" had been borne by human hands, its vaults and buttresses were only the building's external body. Music was the building's inner soul; it was the "supreme manifestation of its existence." At Saint Peter's, however,

Berlioz's Requiem. Jennifer Walker, Oxford University Press. © Oxford University Press 2025.
DOI: 10.1093/9780197688847.003.0005

musical performances required sizable numbers of voices to be even remotely effective. If, for example, the Paris Conservatoire's concert hall regularly held a choir of ninety singers, then Saint Peter's nave required thousands. Berlioz noted only a meager eighteen at Saint Peter's (thirty-two for feast days) and opined that, although such small forces might be adequate for performing Palestrina in the smaller pontifical chapel, even thirty-two singers would be "incapable of producing any effect or even of making itself heard in the largest church in the world."[2]

If Berlioz's early memories of his first communion sparked a sustained interest in the sound world of sacred music, his sonic experiences at Saint Peter's began a career-long obsession with writing grand music for grand spaces. Berlioz heard large-scale music from Lesueur and others, to be sure, but his experiences at Saint Peter's played an even more significant role in how he understood and composed sacred music: only when equal attention was given to sacred texts, the acoustic attributes of the sacred space, and the size of the performing forces could the experience of hearing be sublime. If religious music was open to sonic and textual reconfiguration, as was the case in the *Requiem*, then matching sacred sound with the architectural and acoustic attributes of such performance spaces as Parisian cathedrals was also key in curating an aesthetic of sacred music that could create sublimely sacred aural experiences.

SACRED SPACE AND SACRED SOUND

Berlioz found any *maîtrises* that remained after the closure of choir schools (Notre-Dame's, for example) to be poorly maintained with paltry resources. Until its closure, the only lingering performance space was the Chapelle rcyale, where Lesueur's and Cherubini's sacred works were frequently heard. Though that space attracted the city's most elite performances, it was still insufficient, given that it was "too small to allow them all the developments that the genre entails."[3] And if, as he pointed out, "four thousand Levites were employed in Solomon's temple to sing God's praises," why, then, were performances of grand sacred works relegated to poor performances with minuscule performing forces? The colossal dimensions of Parisian cathedrals demanded musical works of equally imposing scale—it was only under these conditions that a sacred work's full sublimity could be experienced by an audience:

> Have a fine work performed at Notre-Dame by sixty distinguished musicians, and then have the same score rendered by five hundred people picked at random, but competent nonetheless. In the first case, the effect will be meager, paltry, or even nonexistent. In the second, it will be majestic, impressive, sublime.[4]

Berlioz later waxed poetic about the affective possibilities brought about by singing Palestrinian motets with one thousand or twelve hundred voices: "overwhelming" in its effect, the music's harmonic power could only properly be realized when the physical space of the church itself was filled with a mass of voices that was proportionate to its size.[5] He made a similar point in his 1835 review of the performances of Cherubini's *Requiem* at the Invalides chapel and Lesueur's *Te Deum* at Notre-Dame. He bemoaned the lopsided ratio of performers to the dimensions of the performance spaces, writing that the "considerable mass of voices and instruments assembled for great religious ceremonies is still small in relation to the capacity of our places of worship." By contrast, in the much smaller hall of the Conservatoire, the same works and performance forces produced a more profound effect. As he neatly summarized it: "quantity must count more than quality."[6]

This line of thought was not entirely original to Berlioz, however. Anton Reicha, his counterpoint professor at the Conservatoire, had already highlighted the importance of considering acoustic space when formulating the size of performing ensembles in his 1825 *Traité de haute composition musicale.* Like Berlioz, Reicha believed that musical works would be unable to achieve an intended effect if a predetermined ensemble size was ignored in performance.[7] But Lesueur was Berlioz's primary model in this regard. What was, for some critics, a perceived simplicity in Lesueur's compositional style was a careful consideration of sound's relationship to sacred space for Berlioz:

> M. Lesueur takes care to never give a chord less than an entire measure's duration and is always careful to distinguish the nuances of *piano* and *forte* through silences or by using wind instruments. Thanks to his painstaking observance of such rules for sacred music, M. Lesueur has less to fear than other composers from the scantiness of our means of performance and the vastness of our monuments. His music is essentially music for cathedrals. That is where it should be heard and where one can judge it.[8]

Berlioz likewise praised the composer Antoine Elwart for his critical attention to such matters. In a vast and sonorous space like a church, a mindful consideration of space and its relationship to sound was of utmost importance, for it allowed appropriate religious expression to flourish.[9] The *Requiem* provides numerous examples of Berlioz's careful attention to space and sound. The wide intervallic span of the famous flute/trombone paring in the Hostias, so often noted by modern critics for its strangeness and eccentricity, has also been understood as mirroring the unbridgeable space between earthly and heavenly life, heaven and hell, or the land of the living and the souls in Purgatory.[10] Yet the slow-moving progress of the wide pitch spectrum achieves the same effect for which he so admired Lesueur, and his contemporaneous critics rarely, if ever, commented on the passage's unique instrumentation.[11] If, however, the intervallic space is representative of physical space, then Berlioz's melodic line and ascending chordal progressions fills in the material and figurative space left void by orchestrational polarity (see Example 3.1a). And as critics would later notice, silence likewise formed a crucial aspect of Berlioz's understanding of the interactions between space and sound. Strategically placed silences, clearly notated in the score, allowed for the dissipation of sound and a clearer aural experience (Figure 4.1).

Berlioz's concern for adequate attention to the proportional relationship between performance forces and physical space went well beyond a preoccupation with acoustics and a desire for effect. The lackluster performance of Cherubini's *Requiem in C Minor* at Notre-Dame, for example, rendered the attainment of sublimity impossible for the listeners. If the conditions of its performance were so poor that its full effect was unable to be realized, its inadequacy was the result of woefully limited orchestral

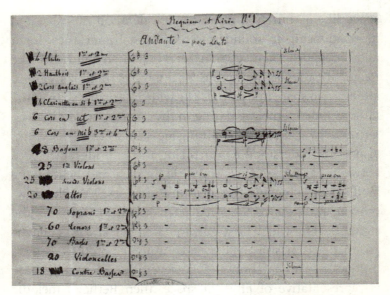

FIGURE 4.1: 1837 manuscript of the Kyrie from the *Requiem*. BnF—Musique MS 1509. Reprinted with permission from the Bibliothèque nationale de France.

capabilities and a general inattention to the incompatibilities of Cherubini's orchestra with Notre-Dame's physical attributes. As Berlioz heard it, the lopsided proportions between space and sound obscured the "sublime totality of the sacred text."[12] In another instance, Berlioz explained that a listener hearing a Beethoven trio in a small space would "gradually feel themselves invaded by a kind of disquiet; they will then experience a deep and intense joy that alternately disturbs them or plunges them into a state of serene delight or veritable ecstasy." Replacing the intimacy of the smaller space with a larger venue would create a sonic experience marked by a certain rational coolness: "he admires the work, but rationally, no longer carried away by irresistible feeling."[13] It is no coincidence that a significant amount of Berlioz's commentary on the matter coincided closely with the composition and first performance of the *Requiem*. Space, for Berlioz, was an agent of the sublime. Sublime transcendence could only be attained when the physical space itself was commensurate with the number of performing bodies.

Berlioz's preoccupation with the acoustic qualities of sacred music stood in opposition to the stylistically and compositionally prescriptive parameters that shaped contemporaneous debates as to how French sacred music should be composed. His 1834 critique of a musical service at the Sistine Chapel, for example, began by outlining the various acoustic missteps that marred the performance. It was not the suitability of the repertoire in question for sacred performance that catalyzed such a "scandalous debasement of religious art"—instead, it was the "great noise" that was created when space and sound were not considered symbiotically that deprived the experience of a necessary sacrality.[14] Berlioz considered a work sacred not by means of its compositional style, but rather by means of the way that it *sounded* in a sacred space:

> The air within the church is struck from so many points at once, in surface and in depth, that it vibrates as a whole and its disturbance develops a power and majesty of action on the human nervous system which the most learned efforts of musical art under ordinary conditions have so far not given us any notion of.[15]

We might think of Berlioz as a nineteenth-century "aural architect." In its simplest manifestation, aural architecture can be defined as the properties of a physical space that can be experienced by listening; it is the composite of numerous surfaces, objects, geometrics, and acoustics in a complicated spatial environment.[16] He drew a direct connection between what he called "monumental music" and architecture; music that embraced this linkage was the most modern in his view.[17] But he also argued that this sort of music must also recognize that architectural space was as much an instrument as the orchestra itself:

> We would never want to persuade ourselves that the building where we make music is a musical instrument itself; that it is to the performers as the body of violins, violas, basses, harps, and pianos is to the strings stretched above it. A correlation between the size and interior configuration of the building and the number of performers is therefore always an absolute necessity.[18]

If, for Berlioz, it might not be easy to think of a structure's edifice as an instrument in the same way as one would an orchestral instrument, the connection is nonetheless necessary: the building is as much an essential element of the performing ensemble as are the strings, tuning pegs, and soundboards of violins and harps. The idea reappeared in force in the *Grand traité d'instrumentation*; Berlioz tells us from the outset that "any sounding body employed by the composer is in fact a musical instrument."[19] And in his review of Choron's funeral, he prefigured the sonic configuration of the *Requiem* through what he heard as the disproportionate relationship between the number of performers, their spatial arrangement, and the physical space of the Invalides chapel:

Two days ago, Choron's many pupils and an orchestra of 130 musicians gathered at the Invalides to perform [Mozart's] requiem mass. . . . The performers, stationed at the highest point in the church, were unable to produce the full effect that such a mass of voices and instruments would have had if they had been placed in tiers, on risers. The sound was lost in certain spaces, and many people complained that they had had difficulty hearing.[20]

While Berlioz reported a positive experience for himself as well as for the listeners seated in the balconies (Berlioz was seated close to the orchestra), he explained that a different spatial arrangement would have enhanced the overall acoustic experience, as would the use of a greater number of instrumentalists and singers. While Mozart, he claimed, was to blame for using only one trombone in the Tuba mirum from his own *Requiem*—"why only one," Berlioz asked, "when thirty or even three hundred would not be too many"—it was the fault of the funeral's organizer that the opportunities offered by the physical space of the Invalides were not utilized to their greatest potential:

The point is that every time the number of musicians fails to correspond exactly to the air mass that is supposed to vibrate, only listeners seated very close to the orchestra can be moved; all others will experience only feeble sensations and fail to grasp the whole or the details. . . . Three hundred performers are not sufficient to carry the harmonies, however broad, through a space as vast as that of the Invalides church. It would take six hundred at the very least. Besides, no one thought to place the voices and instruments on risers, an indispensable precaution on such an occasion.[21]

It was not so much that large spaces demanded a larger number of performers: those performers had to be carefully arranged within the space so that the architectural attributes might be utilized to their fullest potential.

Quantity might have been preferable to quality, but an effective sound depended as much on the specific arrangement of the performing ensemble as it did on its size alone. If Berlioz was clear about how many performers were needed to realize his *Requiem* to its fullest potential, he was even more meticulous as to how they should be situated in the church's nave. His instructions for their placement at the premiere were precise:

> In front of the organ there should be *an amphitheater* or scaffolding in steps for about 200 persons. This number will include *all the singers* and a few instrumentalists. The remainder of the orchestra will be arranged in front of the amphitheater on the horizontal. They can simply be put on the church's floor.[22]

Where, however, were the supplemental brass ensembles to be placed? Before the score's 1838 publication by Maurice Schlesinger, Berlioz added a note that ensured that they would continue to be carefully placed at the four corners of the choral and instrumental arrangement as shown in Figure 4.2. And prior to the release of Giovanni Ricordi's new engraving of the score in 1853, Berlioz added an additional note indicating that the number of performers needed for the entire work was relative and could be doubled or even tripled if the size of the performance space allowed (Figure 4.3). By the time Ricordi's version was published, the *Requiem* had been performed once at the Invalides and thrice at the church of Saint-Eustache—vast acoustic spaces each with their own aural architectures. Berlioz well knew that the idiosyncrasies of the different physical spaces would affect their specific aural architectures and that maintaining the integrity of the *Requiem*'s sound and its ability to transport listeners into a state of sacred sublimity in the larger church of Saint-Eustache would require a larger battery of musicians. Berlioz's notations in later versions of the published score, then, show us just how aware he was of the fluid nature of aural architecture. Even if he never used the phrase "aural architecture," he realized that if the sound sources themselves remained unchanged, the aural architecture always adapted and adjusted with each individual performance.

BUILDING THE REQUIEM AT SAINT-EUSTACHE

The *Requiem* crafted a listening experience that both embraced and transcended the normative boundaries for concert attendance in the nineteenth century. Audiences, in general, did not listen attentively to musical performances, and silence was rare. Critics at multiple performances, however, noted the audience's quiet attentiveness—appropriate, of course, for the liturgical occasions—and their reviews detailed a listening experience that brought the concept of aural architecture into full relief. If, for one critic, Berlioz had asked for too many musicians, he was, according to another writer, right to ask for "a thousand musicians" for the premiere:

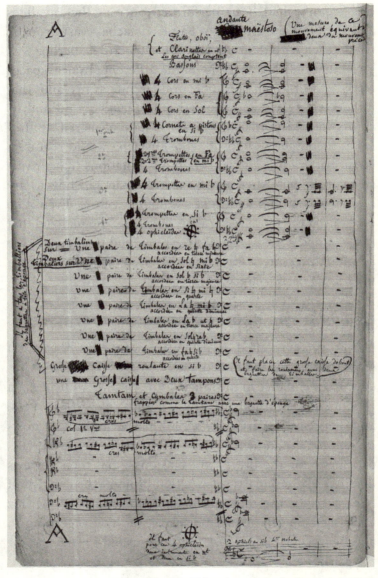

FIGURE 4.2A: 1837 manuscript of the Tuba mirum from the *Requiem*. BnF—Musique MS 1509. Reprinted with permission from the BnF.

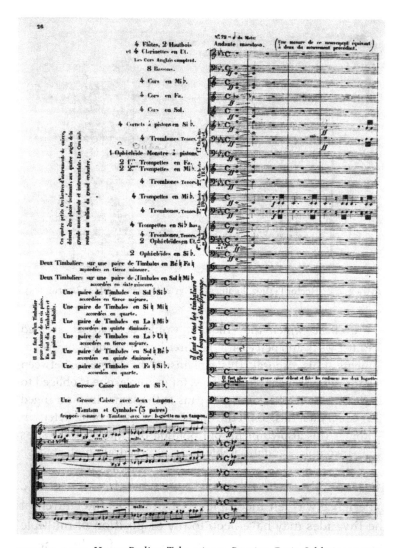

FIGURE 4.2B: Hector Berlioz, Tuba mirum, *Requiem*. Paris: Schlesinger, 1838.

BUILDING THE *REQUIEM*

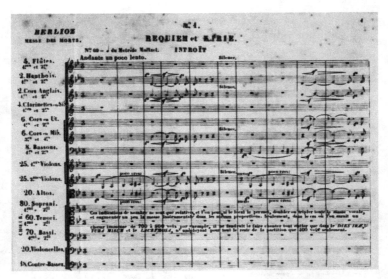

FIGURE 4.3: Hector Berlioz, Requiem et Kyrie, *Requiem*. Milan: Ricordi, 1853.

The effect, which they thought would be colossal, seemed rather weak and petty with the three hundred voices or instruments at his disposal. This explains all the difference between a theater and a church and how, for example, one is obliged to use four orchestras or four organs at the same time, arranged at equal intervals, to fill the immense enclosure of St. Peter's in Rome. This also confirms our opinion that theater orchestras are incomplete and miserable under a cathedral's high arches.

The size of the orchestra was adequate, but this critic's sonic experience was left incomplete. Favorable as the church of the Invalides may have been to the disposition of multiple hundreds of musicians, the draperies used for the funeral ceremonies dampened the sound and thus modified the church's aural architecture. A more complimentary space would have been the dome of the Panthéon, unhampered by the muffling effects of draperies, positioned squarely in the middle of the space's "cross-shaped naves."[23]

The Panthéon may have been preferable to the Invalides to this critic, but the church of Saint-Eustache was the critics' choice when it came to performances of the *Requiem*. Nine years after its premiere, it was heard in full again, this time as part of a ceremony honoring Christoph Willibald Gluck, a composer who had been dead since 1787. An audience of fourteen thousand, drawn from the Parisian elite, packed the church of Saint-Eustache to hear over four hundred musicians perform the *Requiem*. While some critics wondered why Berlioz's requiem mass was performed rather than Mozart's or Cherubini's (Gluck's more immediate contemporaries), the performance was reviewed positively. Critics likewise noted that the vast proportions of both the performance space and the composition of the music itself worked symbiotically to create a truly sacred sound. Absent from critical commentary was any mention of the dramatic, the noisy, or the Romantic. Berlioz's requiem mass, as it was heard at Saint-Eustache, was "a score that bears the best imprint of religious inspiration."[24] Another writer explained that Berlioz's idiosyncratic orchestrations and colossal sound was due directly to the physical attributes of the church in which the work premiered.[25] The combination of sacred sound and sacred space conspired to create an aural experience that "irrefutably proved that the majesty of worship can only draw a new brilliance and power from the aid of musical art deployed in all its pomp."[26] Critics had similar reactions to the playing of the *Requiem* at Saint-Eustache in 1850. Following the catastrophic collapse of a bridge in Angers that killed over two hundred soldiers, the Société Philharmonique staged a charitable performance whose receipts were given to the families of the victims. Writers once again praised the work as a "sublime musical conception." It was not, however, the merit of the music alone that warranted such high praise. Instead, it was the careful consideration of the church's aural architecture that elevated the critic's sonic experience beyond pleasure into sublimity. "We never appreciated [the *Requiem*'s] value more than in the church of Saint-Eustache," he wrote, because its "construction is so favorable to developments in sound. Never before have the trumpets of the Last Judgment so impressed us."[27]

When the *Requiem* was heard for a fourth time at Saint-Eustache in 1852, this time at the funeral of the Baron de Trémont, audiences had an idea of what they might expect. Berlioz was unsurprisingly exacting in his demands for the number of performers and their arrangement in the physical space. As for the singers, there would be five hundred total. Half would sing only in the Tuba mirum and the Lacrymosa; the remaining half sang the entire work. The orchestra, he said, must have 180 performers who would be situated on two platforms that had been laid out in a tiered and sloped semi-circle, and the four brass orchestras would sit at the four corners of the orchestra.[28] This arrangement worked. The critic Léon Kreutzer noted that Berlioz's meticulous attention to the number of performers and their spatial disposition was the reason that he could be praised as the one composer who knew how to draw the fullest and most homogeneous sound from the orchestra—without, as he was careful to add, exceeding the limits of good sense.[29] Other critics noted that, though the vast physical space inside Saint-Eustache might easily have caused an unsettling jumble of sounds, Berlioz avoided this issue through the use of silence. One writer, Joseph-Esprit Duchesne, praised the silences in the Offertoire, for example, and carefully pointed out that the short rest between the statements of "tuba mirum" and "mors stupebit" was necessary not only from an acoustical standpoint, but from a perceptual position as well; the short, five-beat rest and sudden *diminuendo* allowed listeners to aurally reorient themselves. Duchesne's review asked an important question of the *Requiem*: "Are these processes of instrumentation, perfected or invented by Berlioz, only acoustic curiosities? Do they stop only at our ears, or do they make us shudder with enthusiasm and dread and quiver with joy and hope?"[30] Combined with the aural architecture of Saint-Eustache, Berlioz's compositional techniques aligned to create a sonic experience that embodied the sacred sublime despite all their idiosyncrasies.

A concert performance of the *Requiem* in 1900 elicited the most mixed critical reactions. Berlioz, along with Georg Frideric Handel, Charles Gounod, Jules Massenet, Richard Wagner, and Johann Sebastian Bach, appeared on the programs of what was billed as "Les grands oratorios à l'église Saint-Eustache": a large-scale and not uncontroversial series of oratorio performances directed by Eugène d'Harcourt. This performance was smaller in scale and was staged differently: the choir was positioned on raised platforms and positioned with the orchestra under the organ, and the supplemental brass ensembles were placed on either side of the organ tribune and in transverse chapels that faced opposite each other (Figure 4.4). At issue in 1900 was whether the concert performances of works like Handel's

Messiah, Bach's *Saint Matthew Passion*, and Gounod's *Mors et Vita* were appropriate to the building's innately sacred character. By most accounts, Berlioz's *Requiem* was saved by its interrelationship with Saint-Eustache's unique architectural and acoustic environment: indeed, the critic for *La Petite République*, known only as T.M., recognized the *Requiem* as a "masterpiece of musical architecture."[31] Compared to the disastrous performance of Handel's *Messiah* a month earlier—a performance that the vast majority of critics had lambasted for its muddled polyphony and lamentable acoustic effect—the *Requiem* was successfully able to withstand the acoustic challenges of the large space. Though one critic, Henry Boyer, was unable to determine whether it had been Berlioz's orchestration or the use of raised platforms, he nevertheless judged that, with Berlioz, "the acoustics were always better than those of Handel's *Messiah*."[32] For René d'Aral, the church's vast nave had rendered Handel's *Messiah* "devoid of its character." The performance of the work was marred by soloists and vocalists who had "lost their way, so to speak, in a confused murmur that crossed the vast spaces"; moreover, he claimed that Handel's orchestral accompaniment alone was not sufficiently supportive in the space. As for Berlioz's *Requiem*, however, the space worked, and it sounded "admirable in its brilliance under the church's heightened vaults."[33] René Benoist took a similar tack when he compared d'Harcourt's performance to those of Édouard Colonne at the Théâtre du Châtelet in 1894. Whereas the conditions at the Châtelet were "imperfect, given the absolute impossibility of realizing the division of the brass orchestra into four distinct points," those at Saint-Eustache were ideal.[34]

There were, however, those critics who found the performance acoustically lacking. Adolphe Jullien, a prominent critic who otherwise admired the *Requiem* as a "brilliant creation," claimed that "performances of grand religious compositions under the vaults of the church are always flawed because of the echoes that they produce."[35] Moreover, he openly disagreed with Berlioz's belief that cathedrals demanded large numbers of performers: "contrary to Berlioz's ideas, a musical work's effect on the public does not depend at all on the number of musicians charged with its performance."[36] D'Ortigue, too, disagreed with the idea that large spaces required large ensembles. Unsurprisingly, it was plainchant, at least for d'Ortigue, that enjoyed the most favorable acoustic conditions in cathedrals. "Modern" music, in d'Ortigue's view, was unable to deliver the purity of sound for which plainchant had become so revered:

> Plainchant not only harmonizes with the whole of worship and with the ceremonies' imposing gravity. It harmonizes even still with the building's structure. The straightness of the lines that rush from the base toward the summit in an admirable unity goes well with the straightness of this simple melody that climbs the vault. Replace this simple melody with music, that is to say, with the muddle of harmonic parts, the dialogue of instruments, and the diversity of orchestral timbres, [and] the basilica's thousand echoes will respond with such confusion that the musician himself will hardly be able to recognize his work. These delicate combinations, these varied sonorities, these refinements, these learned arrangements that have so much depth in a concert hall or in a chapel . . . are heard in vain in a church.[37]

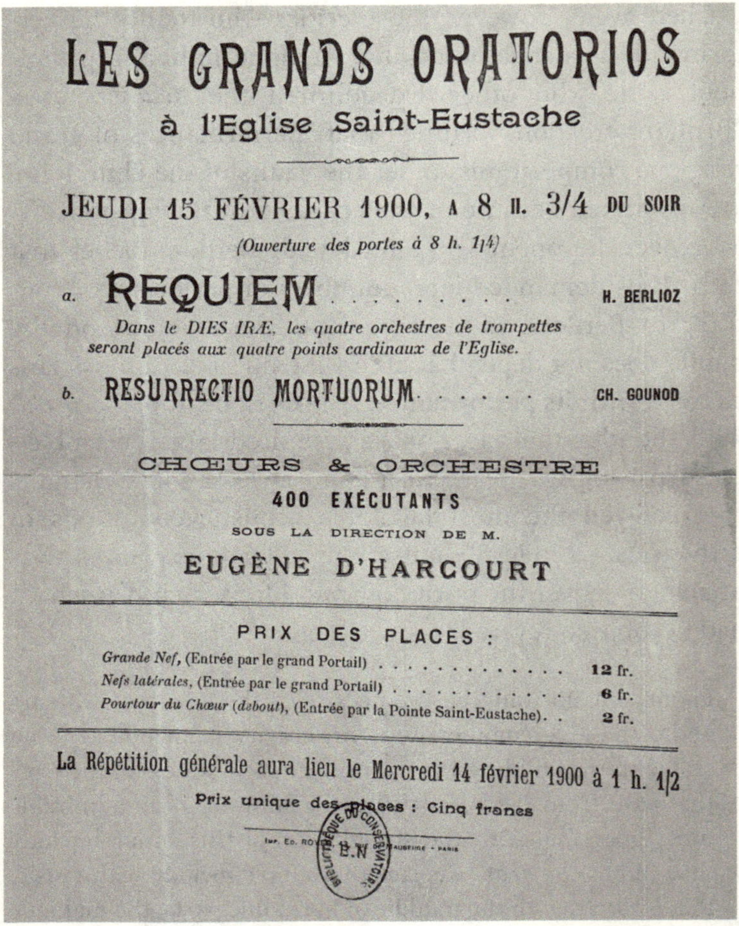

LES GRANDS ORATORIOS

à l'Eglise Saint-Eustache

JEUDI 15 FÉVRIER 1900, A 8 H. 3/4 DU SOIR

(Ouverture des portes à 8 h. 1/4)

a. REQUIEM . . . . H. BERLIOZ

Dans le DIES IRÆ, les quatre orchestres de trompettes seront placés aux quatre points cardinaux de l'Eglise.

b. RESURRECTIO MORTUORUM . . . . . CH. GOUNOD

CHŒURS & ORCHESTRE

400 EXÉCUTANTS

SOUS LA DIRECTION DE M.

EUGÈNE D'HARCOURT

PRIX DES PLACES :

Grande Nef, (Entrée par le grand Portail)	12 fr.
Nefs latérales, (Entrée par le grand Portail)	6 fr.
Pourtour du Chœur (debout), (Entrée par la Pointe Saint-Eustache). .	2 fr.

La Répétition générale aura lieu le Mercredi 14 février 1900 à 1 h. 1/2

Prix unique des places : Cinq francs

FIGURE 4.4: "Les grands oratorios à l'Eglise Saint-Eustache." Program dated February 15, 1900. AHAP Series 2 G 2 1. Reprinted with permission from the AHAP.

D'Ortigue and Jullien found a sympathetic ear in the critic Albert Soubies, who judged acoustic effects in churches to be lacking by virtue of their reverberant echoes and diffusely resonant interiors. For Soubies and the musicologist Charles Malherbe, however, there was a silver lining when it came to the *Requiem*: listening to the *Requiem* at Saint-Eustache, despite its acoustic shortcomings, meant returning the work to its proper musical home. As Malherbe explained it, performing the work at Saint-Eustache was simply the realization of Berlioz's original intentions: it was heard in the "environment for which it had been composed, in church, with an ensemble of means that the author judged necessary to obtain his goal." Theaters or concert halls were incapable of producing the same experiential result. "By conforming to the master's wishes," wrote Malherbe, the conductor and performers thus "realize[d] a manifestation of art that imposes itself onto and will nearly become a revelation to the mass of listeners."[38]

Forty-four years after Berlioz died, Camille Saint-Saëns, a composer who knew Berlioz well, reflected on his many hearings of the *Requiem*. But whereas others leveled the charge of religious indifference at Berlioz, Saint-Saëns took a softer tack. The *Requiem* was undeniably dramatic in his opinion, but not so dramatic as to render it secular: "do not look for Faith and Hope in this work," he wrote. The work was not one that anyone "would dare to call secular," but as he continued, "is it truly religious?" It was, however, religious enough to be at home in Saint-Eustache, especially when compared to theaters like the Châtelet. While

Saint-Saëns found the work to be "at ease" at Saint-Eustache, he found the theater an insufficient alternative by virtue of its theatricality.[39] Hearing the *Requiem* performed at Saint-Eustache created a sonic impression that was wholly unique to the building's architectural qualities—recall Saint-Saëns's vivid description of experiencing the church's pillars as pipes and its edifice as an organ. For Saint-Saëns, the experience of hearing the *Requiem* in sacred spaces was far more powerful than reading the score.

Aural experiences, however powerful, are fleeting. The experience of hearing the *Requiem* at the Invalides in 1837 differed greatly from that of hearing the same work at the church of Saint-Eustache in 1850; listening to a recording of Gustavo Dudamel's performance at Notre-Dame in 2014 does not provide a comparable experience. We hear the same notes and the same chords performed by large masses of instrumentalists and singers, but individual encounters between sound, space, and the body can never be replicated. Recreating the auditory experience of nineteenth-century audiences and critics is impossible. The critical responses to hearing the *Requiem*—particularly at Saint-Eustache—show us that the aural encounter with the work in the nineteenth century was an exceptional one. If the act of analyzing sonic qualities by ear was exceptional for a nineteenth-century listener, this very act was almost a requirement for a successful hearing of the *Requiem*.[40] Berlioz was undoubtedly this type of listener, but he also took great pains to curate this type of listening experience in the *Requiem*. Hearing and understanding sound meant more to Berlioz than superficial understandings of timbre and pitch, for he wanted the hearing subject to be astutely aware of the aural architecture that a space offered.

Berlioz the aural architect thus seemed to have achieved his goal of crafting an aesthetics of sacred music that was equally—if not more—dependent on architectural space than on the particularities of musical composition. We must also remember, however, that aural architecture also carries important sociocultural meanings that often determine the experiential consequences of spatial attributes. In different social settings, acoustic features impart various degrees and types of cultural value. This concept is particularly evident in cathedrals and other sacred spaces. Visual objects, for example, are tangible representations of religious truth in these contexts. The same concept applies to sound. When it came to composing sacred music, Berlioz's creative legitimacy was often determined by his ability to represent religious truth. If he fell short from time to time, so too did others: even Palestrina's music could not occupy the same exalted rank as plainchant if only for the sole reason that the acoustic consequences of contrapuntal writing rendered religious truths inaudible in spaces like Saint-Eustache. If works like the *Requiem* were, at times, criticized as theatrical, the sonic experience that Saint-Eustache offered Parisian listeners registered as religious by virtue of the numerous interactions between acoustic sound and physical space. Modern listeners have noted similar reactions. As one contemporary writer aptly noted following a 2018 performance of the *Requiem* at England's Gloucester Cathedral, "the music seemed to become the 'soul' of the cathedral, as

Berlioz had surely intended."[41] In the *Requiem*, religious truth has been and continues to be heard and understood as an appropriately and legitimately religious thread in the complex fabrics of French aesthetics, theology, and music.

CHAPTER 5

REHEARING
THE REQUIEM

"Berlioz wrote his *Requiem* in a full Romantic fever."[1]

Nearly two hundred years after its premiere, the *Requiem* remains a fixture in the repertoire of orchestras and choirs. Since 2003, it has been performed in its entirety over one hundred times and has appeared on concert programs spanning the globe: from Russia to the United Kingdom, Finland to the United States, and many locations in between. Modern performances have, for the most part, been received positively—but contemporary critics have not always been so kind to Berlioz and his *Requiem*. When, for example, the conductor Édouard Colonne programmed three consecutive performances of the *Requiem* in 1904, the prominent composer Gabriel Fauré responded with annoyance and asked why one would choose to mount a

Berlioz's Requiem. Jennifer Walker, Oxford University Press. © Oxford University Press 2025.
DOI: 10.1093/9780197688847.003.0006

work that, as he heard it, emphasized nothing but its composer's "taste for grand dramatic effects and indifference to the matter of religious music."[2] Fauré's negative assessment of the *Requiem* was but an echo of his own contemporaries: four years earlier, André Suarès, a critic writing in 1900, railed against the inclusion of *Requiem* on the programs to be given at Saint-Eustache. The *Requiem*, he wrote, was nothing more than a "romantic symphony on the Dies irae." Berlioz's greatest flaw was thought to be his sacrifice of religious character for the sake of dramatic effect.[3]

Though the complaints leveled by Fauré and Suarès were largely overshadowed by generally positive critical assessments, they nevertheless fell into a pattern of reception that emerged following late nineteenth- and early twentieth-century performances of the *Requiem*. Jullien, a critic who admired Berlioz, saw in Berlioz and the *Requiem* a greater desire for drama than for religious character—a flaw that was largely the product of the work's trenchant Romanticism.[4] "We must not forget that we are in full Romanticism," wrote Camille Saint-Saëns after hearing it at the Trocadéro in 1912, and an unnamed colleague agreed, claiming that the act of deducing whether Berlioz's inspiration was more dramatic or religious would be futile.[5] And when, in 1904, W. H. Hadow described the *Requiem* as "absolutely unchristian in feeling" by virtue of its "sheer savage force and strength," he did so by painting Berlioz as the arch-Romantic, an artist who, by "subordinating beauty to emphasis," often allowed bursts of white-hot passion and energy to overpower any sense of restraint or self-control. The *Requiem* was merely, as George Bernard Shaw quipped, a "peg to hang his tremendous music on." "To a genuinely religious man," he continued, "the introduction of elaborate sensational instrumental effects into acts of worship would have seemed blasphemous."[6] Orchestral writing like that in the *Requiem* was inherently flawed, for it was only written as such to bolster a narrative or descriptive program—an "extravagant aberration" as Hadow understood it. Berlioz's greatest achievement was, in effect, his Achilles heel: the genius of his idiosyncratic orchestrations was negated by a misplaced desire for dramatic or programmatic effect.[7]

These indictments of the *Requiem* as an insincere work—blasphemous, even—laden with empty effect fall nicely in step with the two predominant claims about Berlioz as a composer of sacred music that have emerged since the late nineteenth century. The first argument holds that Berlioz's indifference to matters pertaining to religion and religious music left him ill-suited to composing sacred music: the *Requiem*, to Anthony Tommasini, the *New York Times'* former chief music critic, "may be most theologically suspect requiem ever written."[8] The second, a corollary to the first, argues that because of this alleged ambivalence to all things religious, the *Requiem* is best understood not as an inherently sacred work, but rather as an exemplar of monumental Romantic grandiosity by virtue of its vast musical proportions, its idiosyncratic orchestrations, and the composer's penchant for dramatic effects. We hear the same story time and time again in statements that locate the proper home for the *Requiem* in concert rather than liturgical performance; it is frequently categorized as closer to drama than to liturgy on a scale from the operatic to the sacred.[9] It is not for nothing that Adolphe Boschot could only describe the *Requiem* as "essentially Romantic."[10]

But if critics writing during Berlioz's lifetime described the *Requiem* as dramatic and theatrical, they often did so in the service of evaluating how it could be heard, understood, and appreciated as genuinely religious. Berlioz's large-scale sacred works—the *Requiem* and, later, the *Te Deum* (1855)—often elicited conflicting opinions about their religious suitability that frequently crossed aesthetic, political, and religious fault lines. For all his well-known conservatism, d'Ortigue nevertheless embraced the *Requiem* as a truly sacred work. Though it was unquestionably a "dramatic" work when compared to plainchant, d'Ortigue's preferred genre of sacred music, he heard qualities in Berlioz's work he still validated as truly religious. D'Ortigue doubled down on his reputation as a hidebound traditionalist in his 1855 review of the *Te Deum*'s premiere at Saint-Eustache. He challenged even the most sincerely Christian composers (among which he could not count Berlioz) to realize a Christian musical expression within the systems of modern tonality, "in its fullness and without blending it with secular expression." It could not be done, d'Ortigue believed, because modern music was unable to deliver the purity of sound for which plainchant had become so revered. And yet he echoed Berlioz's detailed attention to how sacred music should sound in architectural space rather than dwelling on the minutiae of its compositional and stylistic procedures. Despite his misgivings about the encroachment of "modern" sounds and techniques into the inviolate realm of sacred music, he nevertheless reported a positive experience: as with the *Requiem*, Berlioz's personal beliefs and lack of interest in institutionalized religion were not enough to render the *Te Deum* secular.[11] The critic and musicologist Julien Tiersot echoed d'Ortigue's thoughts in his 1895 survey of Berlioz's religious music. He was careful to emphasize Berlioz's lack of faith and his inability to penetrate the liturgical texts at any depth greater than their externally inspirational character, yet he praised the *Requiem* (particularly the Hostias) for its ability to recall sounds of a bygone Christianity; the combinations of low trombones and flutes sounded like "old organs" and produced a "very original archaic" effect.[12] For both d'Ortigue and Tiersot—writers who had vested interests in the aural worlds of French Catholicism—the *Requiem* and the *Te Deum*'s sonic and architectural properties, though troublesome at times, legitimized Berlioz as a composer who possessed the ability to write truly sacred music. Critics may have been mixed on this matter, but often the same critics who recognized that Berlioz was not a traditional Catholic in any sense of the word nevertheless believed the *Requiem* to be sincerely sacred.

Hearings and understandings of the *Requiem* as quintessentially "Romantic" follow a particularly French trend of defining Romanticism as a combination of orchestrational excess, theatrical narrativity, love of effect, and programmaticism. If we accept the violinist and critic Henri Blanchard's 1841 definition of French musical Romanticism as an embrace of large-scale forms and so-called noisy or luxuriant orchestration, then the *Requiem* certainly fits the bill.[13] Berlioz himself is partly to blame for the preponderance of this type of interpretation. Hadow's colorful description of Berlioz as a composer with an imagination always at "white heat" that had never "written with more spontaneous force or with more vehement or volcanic energy" was parroting Berlioz's own recollections of the *Requiem*'s genesis. "I was so wildly intoxicated by the poetry of the *Prose des morts* that my brain could form no clear ideas," recalled Berlioz. "My head was boiling, and I was giddy. Today the eruption is under control, the lava has formed its bed and, with God's help, all will be well."[14] Stripped of its liturgical function and divorced from any contextual nuance, the *Requiem*'s large-scale theatricality delights audiences who have come to expect Berlioz and his music to be the standard-bearer of a certain brand of nineteenth-century Romanticism. We are often primed to hear a liturgical text that has been transformed into a dramatic libretto and to experience music that has been described as representative of God, man, heaven, hell, Purgatory, and a swath of other dramatic, narrative, and programmatic agents. This sort of appeal is not unlike that of other settings of the requiem mass, including those by Giuseppe Verdi and Wolfgang Amadeus Mozart, whose receptions have likewise been shaped by questions that ask what role expressive (or even dramatic) music should play in sacred music and how, if at all, the realms of the secular and the sacred should interact musically. And yet it is precisely this mode of engagement with the *Requiem* as an emblem of the arch-Romantic that leads us to forget that Berlioz's own critics did not hear it as such.

There is no question that the *Requiem* engages with certain facets of Romantic aesthetics and ideology. But to limit our understanding of the work to a short list of hackneyed hermeneutic tropes is to hinder our ability to hear it anew. If a small number of contemporaneous critics indicted Berlioz for crafting a *Requiem* that was too prescriptively programmatic, other critics who experienced sacred sublimity praised him for precisely the opposite. Those writers who argued about the relative merits of certain musics in sacred settings expected the composer to make the sacred nature of the work readily audible through prescribed and easily recognizable musical styles, sounds, and tropes; those who found a certain degree of sacred sublimity or affinity with physical space in the *Requiem* underwent a different type of hermeneutic experience that required a different sort of listener. For all its proximity to sounds, styles, and thought processes that are easy for more modern ears to hear as Romantic, the *Requiem* interacted closely with various contemporaneous discourses that allow us to rehear it in ways that move beyond generic chronological and ideological descriptors. Spurred on by such eye-catching statements as this chapter's epigraph, it is altogether unsurprising that the *Requiem* has fallen into these enticing epistemological traps. But in Berlioz's own moment, the work's so-called effects were less important than its religious ethos, its ability to lead a listener into a state of sublimity, and its ability to interact symbiotically with the sacred spaces in which it was performed. Hearing the *Requiem* anew also invites us to reconsider the numerous ways in which sacred musical works have been effectively secularized as either broadly spiritual or as outliers in their respective composers' overall oeuvres. And yet the *Requiem* invites us to remember that, even if Berlioz did not remain a practicing Catholic in the traditional sense throughout his life, his worldview was not secular, either, for the term does not describe a cultural fabric or an individual constitution that is altogether devoid of religion. If thinking about, listening to, and understanding the work will continue to be an exercise in interpretive hermeneutics—an exercise that was, of course, a favorite of the Romantic generation, it is that same interpretive work that can guide our experiences of the *Requiem* beyond the confines of secularized Romanticism, for the very act of hermeneutic engagement recognizes that there is more to any artistic object than what we hear at first hearing.

ADDITIONAL SOURCES FOR READING AND LISTENING

THE EXISTING SCHOLARSHIP ON Berlioz is extensive, as are the collected editions of Berlioz's correspondence, criticism, and other writings. David Cairns (*Berlioz*, 2 vols., University of California Press, 1999) and Peter Bloom (*The Life of Berlioz*, Cambridge University Press, 1998) have provided meticulously researched yet equally sweeping biographies, while Julian Rushton has studied Berlioz's compositional techniques (and the *Requiem*) in great detail (*The Musical Language of Berlioz*, Cambridge University Press, 1983; *The Music of Berlioz*, Oxford University Press, 2001). Still others have contributed volumes that consider Berlioz's work in specific contexts: its relationship to nineteenth-century Romanticism (Jacques Barzun, *Berlioz and the Romantic Century*, 2 vols., Columbia University Press, 1969), Berlioz and science (Francesca Brittan, *Music and Fantasy in the Age of Berlioz*, Cambridge University Press, 2017), and Berlioz as critic (Katherine Kolb, *Berlioz on Music*, Oxford University Press, 2015; Katharine Ellis, *Music Criticism in Nineteenth-Century France: La Revue et Gazette musicale de Paris, 1834–80*, Cambridge University Press,

1995). Peter Bloom has edited numerous edited collections whose contents also provide indispensable insight into the composer's music and cultural milieu. These include *The Cambridge Companion to Berlioz* (Cambridge University Press, 2000), *Berlioz Studies* (Cambridge University Press, 1992), *Berlioz: Scenes from the Life and Work* (University of Rochester Press, 2008), and *Berlioz: Past, Present, Future* (University of Rochester Press, 2003); his latest collection, *Berlioz in Time: From Early Recognition to Lasting Renown* (University of Rochester Press, 2022), brings together a compendium of his own essays. Notable editions of Berlioz's published writings include, but are not limited to, Peter Bloom's critical edition of the *Memoirs* and Hugh Macdonald's translation of and commentary on the *Grand traité d'instrumentation* (*Berlioz's Orchestration Treatise: A Translation and Commentary*, Cambridge University Press, 2002). A new volume, *Berlioz and His World* (edited by Francesca Brittan and Sarah Hibberd, Chicago University Press, 2024), is also a welcome collection to the vast Berlioz literature. Several analyses of the *Requiem* are of great use including those by Rémy Stricker in *Berlioz dramaturge* (Gallimard, 2003), D. Kern Holoman in *Nineteenth-Century Choral Music* (ed. Donna M. Di Grazia, Routledge, 2013) and *The Cambridge Berlioz Encyclopedia* (ed. Julian Rushton, 2018), and Dominique Hausfater in *Dictionnaire Berlioz* (Fayard, 2003).

For additional information on Catholicism in early nineteenth-century France, Roger Price's *The Church and the State in France, 1789–1870* is key (Palgrave Macmillan, 2017), as is Ralph Gibson's *A Social History of French Catholicism, 1789–1914* (Routledge, 1989). Though her focus is on the uses and understandings of early music in French musical circles, Katharine Ellis's *Interpreting the Musical Past: Early Music in Nineteenth-Century France* (Oxford University Press, 2005) provides an indispensable overview of sacred music during the first half of the nineteenth century; Jean Mongrédien's chapter on sacred music in *French Music from the Enlightenment to Romanticism, 1789–1830* (Amadeus Press, 1986) is also helpful in this regard. The texts on Romanticism as a concept are too numerable to list here, but *The Cambridge Companion to Music and Romanticism* is a good place to start (edited by Benedict Taylor, Cambridge University Press, 2021).

On the topic of the sublime, Philip Shaw's *The Sublime* (2nd ed., Routledge, 2017) is key; also essential is Timothy M. Costelloe's *The Sublime: From Antiquity to the Present* (Cambridge University Press, 2012) and Robert Doran's *The Theory of the Sublime from Longinus to Kant* (Cambridge University Press, 2015). These texts can also be supplemented by the following: Anne Janowitz's entry on the sublime in *A Handbook of Romanticism Studies* (ed. Joel Faflak and Julia M. Wright, Wiley Blackwell, 2012) and Lawrence Kerslake's *Essays on the Sublime: Analyses of French Writings on the Sublime from Boileau to La Harpe* (Peter Lang, 2000). Sarah Hibberd and Miranda Stanyon's edited volume *Music and the Sonorous Sublime in European Culture, 1680–1880* (Cambridge University Press, 2020) is necessary reading on music's relationship with the sublime, as is Stanyon's *Resounding the Sublime: Music in English and German Literature and Aesthetic Theory, 1670–1850* (University of Pennsylvania Press, 2021) and Carmel Raz's article, entitled "Hector Berlioz's Neurophysiological

Imagination," in the *Journal of the American Musicological Society* (Vol. 75, no. 1, 2022).

Barry Blesser and Linda-Ruth Salter's *Spaces Speak, Are You Listening?: Experiencing Aural Architecture* (The MIT Press, 2007) is the foundational text on aural architecture. The collected edition *Music, Space, and Architecture* (edited by Maarten Kloos, Machiel Spaan, and K. J. de Jong, Amsterdam Academy of Architecture, 2012) is also a useful source on the topic. Francesca Brittan's article "The Electrician, The Magician, and the Nervous Conductor" is a wonderful source on Berlioz's theories of musical perception and transmission in large spaces (*Nineteenth-Century Music Review*, Vol. 19, no. 1, 2022), and Inge van Rij's *The Other Worlds of Hector Berlioz: Travels with the Orchestra* (Cambridge University Press, 2015) includes pertinent writing on spatial effect. For a deeper dive into the area of musical architecture, see Deborah Howard and Laura Moretti, *Sound and Space in Renaissance Venice: Architecture, Music, Acoustics* (Yale University Press, 2009). Finally, a discography of notable recordings can be found on the Hector Berlioz Website at http://www.hberlioz.com/music/choral.htm#GMDM.

NOTES

INTRODUCTION

1. DawgFighterz, Reddit post, accessed September 21, 2023, https://www.red dit.com/r/RighteousGemstones/comments/t6y6ss/when_the_reon_title _comes_up_what_is_the_choir/.

2. Jacques Barzun, "Fourteen Points about Berlioz and the Public, or Why There Is Still a Berlioz Problem," in *Berlioz: Past, Present, Future,* ed. Peter Bloom (Rochester, NY: University of Rochester Press, 2003), 193–201.

3. Benedict Taylor, "Defining the Indefinable: Romanticism and Music," in *The Cambridge Companion to Music and Romanticism,* ed. Benedict Taylor (Cambridge: Cambridge University Press, 2021), 3–16.

4. Barzun, "Fourteen Points"; Tom Huizenga, "At 92, The Man Who Wrote the Book on Berlioz Resumes His Case," www.npr.org, March 8, 2019, https:// www.npr.org/sections/deceptivecadence/2019/03/08/691932489/at-92-the-man-who-wrote-the-book-on-berlioz-resumes-his-case.

5. Katharine Ellis, *Music Criticism in Nineteenth-Century France: La Revue et Gazette musicale de Paris, 1834–1880* (Cambridge: Cambridge University Press, 1995), 219–31.

6. Oscar Comettant, "Échos," *Le Siècle,* March 11, 1869; Peter Bloom, *The Life of Berlioz* (Cambridge: Cambridge University Press, 1998), 85–86.

7. Paul Henry Lang, *Music in Western Civilization* (New York: W. W. Norton, 1941), 856–57.

8. Frank Heidlberger, "'Artistic Religiosity': Berlioz between the *Te Deum* and *L'Enfance du Christ,*" in *Berlioz: Scenes from the Life and Work,* ed. Peter Bloom (Rochester, NY: University of Rochester Press, 2008), 26–41.

9. Dominique Hausfater, "Berlioz et l'esthétique de la musique sacrée en France au XIXe siècle," in *Berlioz: textes et contextes,* ed. Joël-Marie Fauquet, Catherine Massip, and Cécile Reynaud (Paris: Société française de musicologie, 2011), 181.

CHAPTER 1

1. Letter from Berlioz to Adèle Berlioz, dated April 17, 1837; printed in Hector Berlioz, *Les Années romantiques 1819–1842* (Paris: Calmann-Lévy, 1904), 339. Emphasis original. All English translations are my own unless otherwise noted. Any that are not my own of Berlioz's correspondence and criticism have been verified against the original texts in either the *CG* or *CM*; any modifications are noted.
2. *Memoirs*, 131–32 [*MémoiresB*, 282].
3. Quoted in Bloom, *The Life of Berlioz*, 85.
4. *Memoirs*, 227 [*MémoiresB*, 428]. Bloom claims that Berlioz's suggested chronology regarding the exact date of receipt is inaccurate.
5. David Cairns, *Berlioz: Servitude and Greatness 1832–1869* (Berkeley: University of California Press, 2000), 140.
6. *Memoirs*, 228 [*MémoiresB*, 429]. Berlioz requested five hundred performers; Gasparin agreed to 430. Letter from Berlioz to his sister Adèle Suat, dated April 17, 1837. *CG* II:344.
7. Letter from Berlioz to his father, Louis-Joseph Berlioz, dated July 29, 1837. *CG* II:360–61.
8. Berlioz to Franz Liszt, dated July 20, 1837. *CG* II:356–57.
9. Berlioz to his mother, Marie-Antoinette-Joséphine Berlioz, dated November 14, 1837. *CG* II:376.
10. Letter from Berlioz to Simon Bernard, the minister of war, dated October 30, 1837. *Nouvelle lettres*, 142–43.
11. See Unsigned, "Ministère de la Guerre: Service solennel d'inhumation de M. le lieutenant-général comte de Damrémont," *Le Journal de Paris*, December 4, 1837; Unsigned, "France. Paris, 5 décembre," *Journal des débats*, December 6, 1837; and X. Y. Z., "Cérémonie des Invalides—Le *Requiem* de Berlioz," *Le Constitutionnel*, December 6, 1837.
12. Unsigned, "France. Paris, 5 décembre."
13. Ibid.
14. Berlioz to his father, Louis-Joseph Berlioz, dated December 7, 1837. *CG* II:383.
15. X. Y. Z., "Cérémonie des Invalides—Le *Requiem* de Berlioz," *Le Constitutionnel*, December 6, 1837.
16. Unsigned, "France. Paris, 6 décembre," *La France*, December 7, 1837. The writer here refers to the grand-croix of the Légion d'honneur.
17. Ibid. See also Berlioz to Humbert Ferrand, dated December 17, 1837. *CG* 2:391.
18. The *Journal de Paris* reprinted the letter sent from Bernard to Berlioz. See *Journal de Paris*, December 9, 1837.
19. Unsigned, "Messe de *Requiem* par Hector Berlioz," *Le Charivari*, December 6, 1837; Unsigned, "France. Paris, 5 décembre"; Th. V., "Revue musicale," *Le Monde dramatique*, December 1837, 381.

20. Joseph d'Ortigue, "D'un arrêté ministériel relatif à une messe en musique," *Journal de Paris*, August 8, 1837.

21. Katharine Ellis, *Interpreting the Musical Past: Early Music in Nineteenth-Century France* (Oxford: Oxford University Press, 2005), 193–97 at 196.

22. Bloom, *The Life of Berlioz*, 83.

23. Unsigned, "Musique—Le Conservatoire—M. Berlioz—Ste. Cécile," *Le Corsaire*, November 24, 1827.

24. Unsigned, "La Messe de M. Berlioz," *Le Figaro*, December 5, 1837. See also J. M . . . er [Joseph Mainzer], "Feuilleton du 12 Octobre," *Le National*, December 12, 1837.

25. Joseph d'Ortigue, "Musique religieuse: Messe de *Requiem* de M. H. Berlioz," *La Quotidienne*, December 6, 1837.

26. Ellis, *Interpreting the Musical Past*, 195–96.

27. Sylvia L'Écuyer, ed. *Joseph d'Ortigue: écrits sur la musique* (Paris: Société française de musicologie, 2003), 543.

28. Bottée du Toulmon, "Du Requiem de M. Berlioz," *Revue et Gazette musicale*, December 10, 1837, 531–35.

29. *Journal des débats*, December 6, 1837.

30. Adolphe Boschot, *Un romantique sous Louis-Philippe* (Paris: Plon, 1908), 357.

31. Bernard's letter to Berlioz was reprinted in the *Journal de Paris*, December 9, 1837.

32. J. M . . . er [Joseph Mainzer], "Feuilleton du 12 Octobre."

CHAPTER 2

1. Bottée du Toulmon, "Du Requiem de M. Berlioz," *Revue et Gazette musicale de Paris*, December 10, 1837, 534.

2. *BoM* (companion website), 1 [*Le Correspondant*, April 21, 1829].

3. *Memoirs*, 31–32 [*MémoiresB*, 127].

4. *Memoirs*, 181 [*MémoiresB*, 356].

5. *Memoirs*, 182 [*MémoiresB*, 357].

6. David Cairns, "Religion," in *The Cambridge Berlioz Encyclopedia*, ed. Julian Rushton (Cambridge: Cambridge University Press, 2018), 275.

7. *Memoirs*, 227 [*MémoiresB*, 429 n. 2].

8. Michael McClellan and Simon Trezise, "The Revolution and Romanticism to 1848," in *The Cambridge Companion to French Music*, ed. Simon Trezise (Cambridge: Cambridge University Press, 2015), 114.

9. Roger Price, *The Church and the State in France, 1789–1870* (Aberystwyth: Palgrave Macmillan, 2017).

10. Jean Mongrédien, *French Music from the Enlightenment to Romanticism, 1789–1830*, trans. Sylvain Frémaux (Portland, OR: Amadeus Press, 1996 [1986]), 159–65.

11. *BoM*, 86 [*Revue et Gazette musicale de Paris*, September 7, 1834]. See also Ellis, *Interpreting the Musical Past*, 9.

12. Alexandre-Étienne Choron, "Mémoire sur la situation actuelle de la Musique Religieuse et sur les moyens d'en opères la restauration." BnF-Musique Res. F 1665 (12).

13. Berlioz, "Concert de Mlle Mazel à l'Hôtel-de-Ville," *Revue et Gazette musical de Paris*, July 10, 1836, 243; Katharine Ellis, "Vocal Training at the Paris Conservatoire and the Choir Schools of Alexandre-Étienne Choron: Debates, Rivalries, and Consequences," in *Musical Education in Europe (1770–1914): Compositional, Institutional, and Political Changes*, ed. Michael Fend and Michel Noiray, Vol. 1 (Berlin: Berliner Wissenschafts-Verlag, 2005), 125–44.

14. Étienne Jardin, "Les Concerts d'Alexandre Choron," in *Musiques et pratiques religieuses en France au XIXᵉ siècle*, ed. Fanny Gribenski and Amélie Porret-Dubreuil (Paris: Classiques Garnier, 2022), 229–47.

15. *BoM*, 83 [*Le Rénovateur*, August 11, 1834]. Translation modified from Rosenberg's.

16. *BoM*, 86 [*Revue et Gazette musicale de Paris*, September 7, 1834].

17. *BoM* (companion website), 2 [*Le Correspondant*, April 21, 1829].

18. Ralph P. Locke, "The Religious Works," in *The Cambridge Companion to Berlioz*, ed. Peter Bloom (Cambridge: Cambridge University Press, 2000), 99.

19. Letter from Berlioz to Lesueur, dated July 1824. *CG* I: 60.

20. *BoM* (companion website), 3 [*Le Correspondant*, April 21, 1829].

21. Ellis, *Interpreting the Musical Past*, 193–97.

22. *CM* III: 143.

23. Hector Berlioz, *Evenings with the Orchestra*, trans. Jacques Barzun (Chicago: University of Chicago Press, 1999), 190–92.

24. See also Hector Berlioz, "On Church Music," in *The Art of Music and Other Essays (A travers chants)*, trans. and ed. Elizabeth Csicsery-Rónay (Bloomington: Indiana University Press, 1994), 172–75.

25. Alban Ramaut, "Aesthetics (1)," in *The Cambridge Berlioz Encyclopedia*, ed. Julian Rushton (Cambridge: Cambridge University Press, 2017), 2–3.

26. David Charlton, "Learning the Past," in *Berlioz; Past, Present, Future*, ed. Peter Bloom (Rochester, NY: University of Rochester Press, 2003), 34–56; Julian Rushton, "Berlioz's *Messe solennelle* and His Debt to Lesueur: Ecstasy of Emulation," *Musical Times* 140, no. 1868 (Autumn 1999): 11–18.

27. Mona Ozouf, "De-Christianization," in *A Critical Dictionary of the French Revolution*, ed. François Furet and Mona Ozouf (Cambridge, MA: Belknap Press of Harvard University Press, 1989), 20–32.

CHAPTER 3

1. Ernest Dubreuil, "Paris," *Messager des Théatres et des Arts*, October 24, 1852.
2. Robert Doran, *The Theory of the Sublime from Longinus to Kant* (Cambridge: Cambridge University Press, 2015), 110–14.
3. Sarah Hibberd and Miranda Stanyon, "Sonorous Sublimes: An Introduction," in *Music and the Sonorous Sublime in European Culture, 1680–1880*, ed. Sarah Hibberd and Miranda Stanyon (Cambridge: Cambridge University Press, 2020), 1–25.
4. Aubin-Louis Millin, *Dictionnaire des beaux-arts*, Vol. 3 (Paris: Desray, 1806), 603.
5. Katherine Kolb Reeve, "Primal Scenes: Smithson, Pleyel, and Liszt in the Eyes of Berlioz," *19th-Century Music* 18, no. 3 (Spring 1995): 211–35; Katharine Ellis, "Berlioz, the Sublime, and the *Broderie* Problem," in *Hector Berlioz: Miscellaneous Studies*, ed. Fulvia Morabito and Michela Niccolai (Bologna: Ut Orpheus Edizioni, 2005), 29–59.
6. Cairns, *Berlioz*, Vol. 1, 96, 171, 457. See also *BoM*, 136 [March 1, 1835]; Reeve, "Primal Scenes."
7. *Treatise*, 201 [*NBE* 24, 302]. All English translations from the *Treatise* are borrowed from Hugh Macdonald, *Berlioz's Orchestration Treatise: A Translation and Commentary* (Cambridge: Cambridge University Press, 2002).
8. *Treatise*, 289 [*NBE* 24, 488].
9. Ellis, "Berlioz, the Sublime, and the *Broderie* Problem."
10. Letter from Berlioz to Albert Du Boys dated July 20, 1825, *CG* I: 95–96.
11. Letter from Berlioz to Humbert Ferrand dated November 29, 1827, *CG* I: 159–60.
12. *Memoirs*, 479 [*MémoiresB*, 798].
13. *CM* III: 360–61.
14. *Memoirs*, 479 [*MémoiresB*, 798].
15. Hibberd and Stanyon, "Sonorous Sublimes: An Introduction," 22.
16. *MémoiresB*, 430 n.12.
17. Lawrence Kerslake, *Essays on the Sublime: Analyses of French Writings on the Sublime from Boileau to La Harpe* (Bern: Peter Lang: 2000).
18. Jacques-Bénigne Bossuet, *Œuvres complètes*, Vol. 10 (1867), 120.
19. See *BoM*, 107 [*Le Rénovateur*, November 16, 1834] for Berlioz's citation of Bossuet's grand style.
20. Sophie Hache, "Thunder or Celestial Harmony: French Theological Debates on the Sonorous Sublime," in *Music and the Sonorous Sublime*, 26–43, at 31.
21. *BoM* (companion website), 1 [*Le Correspondant*, April 21, 1829]; and *BoM*, 253 [*Journal des débats*, September 18, 1836].
22. *BoM* (companion website), 2 [*Le Correspondant*, April 21, 1829]. Translation adapted from Rosenberg's.

23. Unsigned, "France. Paris, 5 décembre," *Journal des débats*, 6 December 1837.
24. E. Duchesne [likely Joseph-Esprit Duchesne], "Requiem de M. Berlioz, exécutée en l'honneur de M. le Baron de Trémont," *Journal des débats*, November 23, 1852. See also Alphonse de Calonne, "Revue musicale," *Le Dix décembre*, May 14, 1850.
25. Unsigned, "Cérémonie funèbre en l'honneur de la mémoire de M. le Baron de Trémont," *L'Éclaireur de l'arrondissement de coulommiers*, November 14, 1852; Dubreuil, "Paris."
26. Unsigned, "Messe de Requiem par Hector Berlioz," *Le Charivari*, December 6, 1837.
27. Ibid.
28. Duchesne, "Requiem de M. Berlioz."
29. Léon Kreutzer, "Revue musicale," *La Quotidienne*, August 28, 1846; Kreutzer, "*Le Requiem* de Berlioz," *Revue et Gazette musicale de Paris*, October 31, 1852, 370.
30. J. M . . . er, [Joseph Mainzer] "Feuilleton du 12 octobre," *Le National*, December 12, 1837.
31. Alphonse de Calonne, "Revue musicale."
32. See, e.g., Unsigned, "Messe de Requiem par Hector Berlioz."
33. Quoted in Léon Vallas, "Un concert Berlioz à Lyon en 1845," *Revue musicale de Lyon*, November 25, 1906, 206.

CHAPTER 4

1. Camille Saint-Saëns reflected upon his hearing of the *Requiem* in 1852 in Unsigned, "Discours de M. Saint-Saëns lu par M. le Maire de la Côte-Saint-André," *Le Guide musical*, 6 and 13 September 6 and 13, 1903, 627.
2. *Memoirs*, 181–82 [*MémoiresB*, 356].
3. *BoM* (companion website), 4 [*Le Correspondant*, April 21, 1829].
4. Ibid., 5.
5. *BoM*, 88 [*Revue et Gazette musicale de Paris*, September 7, 1834].
6. *BoM* (companion website), 4 [*Le Correspondant*, April 21, 1829]. The translation here is adapted from Rosenberg's.
7. Anton Reicha, *Traité de haute composition musicale*, Vol. 2 (Paris: Zetter, 1825), 329.
8. *CM* III: 306.
9. *CM* III: 397.
10. Rosa E. Lewis, "Hector Berlioz's Religious Ambivalence and Its Impact on His Music" (MA thesis, University of Hawai'i, 2000); David Cairns, *Berlioz*, Vol. 2, 137; Cone, "Berlioz's Divine Comedy," 7.

11. Jennifer Walker, "Hearing the Hostias, Rehearing the *Requiem*," in *Berlioz and His World*, ed. Francesca Brittan and Sarah Hibberd (Chicago: Chicago University Press, 2024), 115–25.
12. *BoM*, 173–74 [*Journal des débats*, August 9, 1835].
13. Berlioz, *The Art of Music and Other Essays*, ed. and trans. Elizabeth Csicsery-Ronay, 60–61.
14. *CM* I: 239–40.
15. Berlioz, *Evenings with the Orchestra*, trans. Barzun, 233.
16. Barry Blesser and Linda-Ruth Salter, *Spaces Speak: Experiencing Aural Architecture* (Cambridge, MA: MIT Press, 2007), 5, 2.
17. Letter from Berlioz to Louis Berlioz, dated September 8, 1842, *Nouvelles lettres*, 201.
18. Berlioz, "Revue musicale: fêtes musical de Toulouse," *Le Rénovateur*, July 19, 1835.
19. *Treatise*, 2 [*NBE* 24, 5].
20. *BoM*, 83–84 [*Le Rénovateur*, August 11, 1834].
21. *BoM*, 88–89 [*Revue et Gazette musicale de Paris*, September 7, 1834.
22. Letter from Berlioz to Jean Vatout dated October 30, 1837, *CG* II: 373. Emphasis original.
23. X.Y.Z., "Cérémonie des Invalides—Le Requiem de M. Berlioz," *Le Constitutionnel*, December 6, 1837; L.V. [Louis Viardot], "Requiem de M. Berlioz," *Le Siècle*, December 6, 1837.
24. Maurice Bourges, "Requiem en l'honneur de Gluck," *Revue et gazette musicale*, August 23, 1846, 270.
25. Léon Kreutzer, "Revue musicale," *La Quotidienne*, August 28, 1846.
26. Unsigned, "Messe de Requiem en l'honneur de Gluck," *Journal des débats*, September 11, 1846.
27. F.B., "Grande Société philharmonique de Paris: *Requiem* de M. Berlioz," *Messager des théâtres et des arts*, May 14, 1850.
28. Joël-Marie Fauquet, "Hector Berlioz et l'Association des Artistes Musiciens: lettres et documents inédits," *Revue de musicologie* 67, no. 2 (1981): 224.
29. Léon Kreutzer, "Le *Requiem* de Berlioz," *Revue et gazette musicale*, October 31, 1852, 370.
30. E. Duchesne, [Joseph-Esprit], "Requiem de M. Berlioz, exécutée en l'honneur de M. le Baron de Trémont," *Journal des débats*, November 23, 1852.
31. T. M., "Courrier des théâtres," *La Petite République*, February 18, 1900.
32. Henry Boyer, "Grands concerts," *Le Courrier du soir*, February 20, 1900.
33. René d'Aral, "Le *Requiem* de Berlioz à Saint-Eustache," *Le Gaulois*, February 16, 1900.

34. René Benoist [Des Tournelles], "Les Grands Oratorios à l'Église Saint-Eustache," *Le Moniteur universel*, February 16, 1900.

35. Adolphe Jullien, "Revue musicale: Hændel à Saint-Eustache," *Le Moniteur universel*, January 29, 1900; Jullien, *Hector Berlioz, sa vie et ses œuvres* (Paris: Librairie de l'art, 1888), 105.

36. Jullien, "Revue musicale," *Le Moniteur universel*, February 26, 1900.

37. Joseph d'Ortigue, "L'Année 1855 au point de vue de la musique religieuse," *Revue de musique ancienne et moderne* (1856): 67.

38. Albert Soubies [B. de Lomagne], "Le *Requiem* de Berlioz à Saint-Eustache," *Le Soir*, February 17, 1900; Charles Malherbe, Program Booklet, February 15, 1900, AHAP, Musique sacrée (concerts au Saint-Eustache), Series 2 G 2 1.

39. Camille Saint-Saëns, "Le *Requiem* de Berlioz," *École buissonnière* (Paris: Pierre Lafitte, 1913), 209, 213.

40. See Julia Kursell, "Hearing in the Music of Hector Berlioz," in *Nineteenth-Century Opera and the Scientific Imagination*, ed. David Tippett and Benjamin Walton (Cambridge: Cambridge University Press, 2019), 109–33.

41. Haydn Greenway, "Berlioz *Requiem* at the Cheltenham Music Festival," The Hector Berlioz Website, accessed September 20, 2023, www.hberlioz.com/others/reviews2018.htm.

CHAPTER 5

1. Unsigned and undated press clipping, Berlioz (Hector): Requiem, divers auditions, BnF-Arts du spectacle, 8-RO-2465.

2. Gabriel Fauré, "Les Concerts," *Le Figaro*, January 25, 1904.

3. Litte [André Suarès], "Les Grands concerts," *La Republique française*, February 18, 1900.

4. Jullien, *Hector Berlioz, sa vie et ses œuvres*, 104.

5. Camille Saint-Saëns, "Le Requiem de Berlioz" and an unsigned and undated press clipping, both found in Berlioz (Hector): Requiem, divers auditions, BnF-Arts du spectacle, 8-RO-2465.

6. George Bernard Shaw, *The Great Composers: Reviews and Bombardments* (Berkeley: University of California Press, 1978), 26.

7. W. H. Hadow, "Hector Berlioz," in *Grove's Dictionary of Music and Musicians*, ed. J. A. Fuller Maitland, Vol. 1 (London: Macmillan, 1904), 315.

8. Anthony Tommasini, "A Soaring Requiem to Fill St. Paul's," *New York Times*, June 27, 2012.

9. Julian Rushton, *The Music of Berlioz* (Oxford: Oxford University Press, 2001), 40; Bloom, *The Life of Berlioz*, 83, 192.

10. Adolphe Boschot, "La Musique religieuse de Berlioz," BnF-Arts du Spectacle, 8-RO-2528, 1173.

11. Joseph d'Ortigue, "L'année 1855 au point de vue de la musique religieuse," *Revue de musique ancienne et moderne* (1856): 65–79; d'Ortigue, "Le *Te Deum* de M. Hector Berlioz," *Journal des débats*, May 26, 1855.

12. Julien Tiersot, "Berlioz, compositeur de musique religieuse: le *Requiem* et le *Te Deum*," *Le revue bleue*, April 20, 1895, 500–3.

13. Ellis, *Music Criticism in Nineteenth-Century France*, 161–62 and 222–23.

14. *Selected Letters of Berlioz*, 142. See also *Memoirs*, 228 [*MémoiresB*, 430].

INDEX

For the benefit of digital users, indexed terms that span two pages (e.g., 52–53) may, on occasion, appear on only one of those pages.

Figures are indicated by *f* following the page number.

1830 July Revolution, 8–10

acoustics
  Berlioz's attention to as a
    composer, 78, 80–81, 86–87,
    92–93, 98–100
  Berlioz's experiences of as a
    listener, 77–83, 84–86
  and debates over sacred music,
    83, 95–98
  and reception of the *Requiem*,
    90–95, 97–100
Alizard, Adolphe-Joseph-Louis,
  15–16
Ancelin, Abbé, 18–19
art-religion, 43–44, 55–56
audiences, 25–27, 45–46, 59–61, 87,
  98–99
aural architecture, 83–87, 92–93,
  98–100. *See also* acoustics

Bach, Johann Sebastian, 93–94
Barzun, Jacques, 3–4

Beethoven, Ludwig van, 22–24,
  48–50, 81–83
Benoist, René, 93–94
Berlioz, Hector
  on the 1830 July Revolution, 10
  and acoustics as a composer, 78,
    80–81, 86–87, 92–93, 98–100
  and acoustics as a listener, 77–83,
    84–86
  aesthetic of sacred music, 41–44,
    58–59, 74–76, 98–100. 104–5
  as aural architect, 83–87, 92–93,
    98–100
  encounters with sacred music,
    28–30, 39–40, 77–78
  L'Enfance du Christ, 4–5
  fighting for payment, 12–14
  Messe solennelle, 21–22. 29–30,
    50–51, 53–55, 58–59, 52–63
  perceived as excessive
    Romantic, 3–7, 60–61, 74–76,
    102–3, 105–6
  political views of, 9–10

Berlioz, Hector (*cont.*)
  relationship to Catholicism, 4–6,
    21–24, 28–30, 36–38, 41–44,
    104–8
  reputation of, 9–10, 20–22, 60–61,
    101–8
  on the *Requiem*, 8, 16–18, 51–53,
    86, 105–6
  on sacred music, 28–30, 34–41,
    58–59
  Les Soirées de l'orchestre, 40–41
  Te Deum, 3–6, 104–5
  view of the sublime, 36–38, 43–
    44, 48–55, 58–59, 74–76
  See also *Requiem* (*Grande Messe
    des morts*)
Bernard, Simon, 13, 18–19, 25–27
biohermeneutics, 3–6
Blanchard, Henri, 105–6
Bloom, Peter, 3–4
Boileau, Nicolas, 47–50, 55–57
Boschot, Adolphe, 24–25, 103
Bossuet, Jacques-Bénigne, 56–59
Bottée de Toulmon, Auguste, 24–27
Boyer, Henry, 93–94
Burke, Edmund, 46–47, 55, 56–57,
  62–63, 66–67

Cairns, David, 29–30
Calonne, Alphonse de, 62–63
Castil-Blaze (François-Henri-
  Joseph Blaze), 34–35
Catholicism
  after the French Revolution,
    30–31, 41–43
  Berlioz's relationship to, 4–6,
    21–24, 28–30, 36–38, 41–44,
    104–8
  d'Ortigue on, 19–21, 22–25
  and the sublime, 55–60, 62–65
  See also sacred music
Cavé, Edmond, 11–13

Chapelle royale (Tuileries Chapel),
  31–33
Charivari, Le (magazine), 18–19
Cherubini, Luigi
  Berlioz commissioned over, 11–13,
    20–21
  at the Chapelle royale, 31–32,
    78–79
  Requiem in C Minor, 8, 16–18,
    20–21, 61–62, 79–80, 81–83,
    91–92
Choron, Alexandre-Étienne, 33–38
church choir schools. See *maîtrises*
Clément, Félix, 38–39
Colonne, Édouard, 93–94, 101–2
Comettant, Oscar, 3–4
Constitutionnel, Le (newspaper),
  16–18
Corsaire, Le (newspaper), 21–22

Dalayrac, Nicolas, 29–30, 33–34,
  39–40
Damrémont, Comte de (Charles-
  Marie Denys), 13–14
Danjou, Félix, 38–39
d'Aral, René, 93–94
Davis, Sir Colin, 3–4
d'Harcourt, Eugène, 93–94
d'Ortigue, Joseph, 19–25, 38–39,
  58–59, 73–74, 95, 104–5
Dubreuil, Ernest, 59–60
Duchesne, Joseph-Esprit, 92–93
Dudamel, Gustavo, 98–99
Dupont, Alexis, 15–16
Duprez, Gilbert, 15–16

Elwart, Antoine, 80–81
Enfance du Christ, L' (Berlioz), 4–6
excess, trope of, 2–7, 22–24, 48–50,
  101–3, 105–6
expressiveness, 3–4, 24–25, 37–44,
  58–59, 105–6

Fauré, Gabriel, 101–2
Fieschi, Giuseppe-Maria, 9
Figaro, Le (newspaper), 22–24
French Revolution, 30–31, 41–43

Gasparin, Comte Adrien de, 10–12, 13
Gloucester Cathedral, 99–100
Gluck, Christoph Willibald, 91–92
Gossec, François-Joseph, 16–18
Gounod, Charles, 93–94
grand motet, 30–31, 32–33

Habeneck, François-Antoine, 15–16
Hadow, W. H., 102–3, 105–6
Handel, Georg Frideric, 93–94
Hélène of Mecklenburg, Princess,
    12–13
Herold, Ferdinand, 18–19

insincerity, trope of, 2–6, 19–20,
    22–24, 101–3
Institution Royale de musique
    religieuse, 33–36
Invalides chapel. *See*
    Saint-Louis-des-Invalides

Joinville, Prince de, 8–9
Journal des débats, 16, 24–25
Jullien, Adolphe, 95, 102–3
July Monarchy, 8–10, 41–43

Kant, Immanuel, 46–47, 53–55
Kreutzer, Léon, 61–62, 92–93

Lang, Paul Henry, 4–6
Lesueur, Jean-François, 31–33,
    37–38, 41–43, 51–55, 78–81
Levasseur, Nicolas-Prosper, 15–16
listeners. *See* audiences
Longinus, 46–48, 53–55, 56–59,
    62–63
Louis-Philippe, King, 8–10, 32–33

Mainzer, Joseph, 22–24, 25–27,
    62–63
maîtrises (church choir schools),
    30–31, 32–33, 34–35, 78–79
Malherbe, Charles, 97
Méhul, Étienne-Nicolas, 31–32
Messe solennelle (Berlioz), 21–22,
    29–30, 50–51, 53–55, 58–59,
    62–63
Millin, Aubin-Louis, 48–50
Monde dramatique, Le (journal),
    18–19
Mortier, Édouard-Adolphe, 9
Mozart, Wolfgang Amadeus, 2–3, 8,
    16–18, 22–24, 61–62, 85, 91–92,
    105–6

Napoleon Bonaparte, 30–32
Napoléon III, 41–43
National, Le (newspaper), 22–24
Nemours, Duke of, 8–9
Notre-Dame de Paris, 32–33, 38–39,
    78–80, 81–83, 98–99

Orleans, Duke of, 8–9, 12–13, 14–15,
    18–19

Paisiello, Giovanni, 31–32
Palestrina, Giovanni Luigi da,
    22–24, 41, 70–72, 77–78, 79–80,
    99–100
Panthéon, 90–91
Paris Conservatoire, 21–22, 34–35,
    77–78, 79–80
Petite République, La (newspaper),
    93–94
Pius VII, Pope, 30–31
plainchant
    Berlioz's criticism of, 40–41
    Choron's criticism of, 33–34
    d'Ortigue's advocacy for, 20–21,
    22–24, 38–39, 58–59, 95, 104–5

plainchant (*cont.*)
  heard in the *Requiem*, 20–21,
    22–24, 25–27, 63–65

Reicha, Anton, 80
religious terror, 20–21, 45, 48. *See
  also* sublimity
Renaissance polyphony, 22–24,
  38–39. *See also* Palestrina,
  Giovanni Luigi da
Requiem (Grande Messe des morts)
  (Berlioz)
  Agnus Dei, 16–18
  Berlioz on, 8, 16–18, 51–53, 86,
    105–6
  cancellation of July 1837
    performance, 12–13
  commissioning of, 9–14
  Confutatis, 67–70
  Dies irae, 59–61, 62–65
  as excessive or insincere, 2–7,
    19–20, 22–24, 101–3, 105–6
  Hostias, 24–27, 48–50, 52–53*f*,
    80–81, 104–5
  Lacrymosa, 22–24, 70–72, 92–93
  modern performances of, 98–100,
    101–2
  Offertory, 22–24, 70–74, 74*f*, 75*f*,
    92–93
  performance spaces for, 14–16,
    86–100, 106–8
  performing forces for, 12–14,
    15–18, 59–61, 87–93
  plainchant heard in, 20–21,
    22–24, 25–27, 63–65
  premiere of (December 5, 1837),
    14–20, 22–27, 86–91
  published scores of, 86–87
  Quaerens me, 22–24, 53–55,
    70–72, 72*f*
  Quid sum miser, 53–55, 63–67, 65*f*
  Recordare, 66, 67–70

Requiem et Kyrie, 82*f*, 90*f*
  reworking of the *Messe solennelle*
    in, 53–55
Rex tremendae, 2–3, 4–6, 67–70,
  68–69*f*, 70*f*, 71*f*
  and Romanticism, 3–7, 24–27,
    43–44, 102–8
  and sacred music, 4–6, 18–27,
    59–62, 74–76, 99–100, 101–8
  Sanctus, 15–16, 18–19
  space and sound in, 80–81, 86–87
  staging of, 14–16, 86–87, 92–94
  as sublime, 45–46, 48, 51–55,
    59–65, 66–76, 106–8
  Tuba mirum, 53–55, 59–60,
    63–65, 88–89*f*, 92–93
  used in *The Righteous Gemstones*,
    1–3, 4–6
Revolutionary hymns, 31–32
Revue et Gazette musicale de Paris,
  3–4, 24–27, 36–37
Righteous Gemstones, The (HBO
  series), 1–3, 4–6
Romanticism, 3–7, 18–19, 24–27,
  43–44, 102–8
Rossini, Gioachino, 11–12

sacred music
  and acoustics, 77–83, 91–100
  Berlioz on, 28–30, 34–41, 58–59
  Berlioz's aesthetic of, 41–44,
    58–59, 74–76, 98–100, 104–5
  Berlioz's encounters with, 28–30,
    39–40, 77–78
  debates on, 18–27, 38–39, 40–44,
    58–59, 83, 95–98, 104–5
  decline of, 30–37
  expressive potential of, 24–25,
    37–44, 58–59, 105–6
  Gasparin's support for, 10–12
  influence of secular genres on,
    22–24, 33–34, 39–40, 104–6

and the *Requiem*'s reception, 4–6,
  18–27, 59–62, 74–76, 99–100, 101–8
and Romanticism, 43–44, 102–8
and the sublime, 36–38, 55–60,
  62–65, 66–76, 106–8
See also Catholicism; plainchant
Sain d'Arod, Prosper, 73–74
Saint Peter's basilica (Rome), 77–78
Saint-Eustache, 39–40, 86–87,
  91–99, 96f, 101–2
Saint-Louis-des-Invalides, 10–11,
  13, 14–19, 79–80, 84–85, 86–87,
  90–91, 98–99
Saint-Saëns, Camille, 97–98, 102–3
Schneitzhoeffer, Jean, 15–16
Shaw, George Bernard, 102–3
simplicity, 47–48, 55
Sistine Chapel, 83
Société Philharmonique, 91–92
Soirées de l'orchestre, Les (Berlioz),
  40–41
Soubies, Albert, 97
Stoltz, Rosine, 15–16
Suarès, André, 101–2
sublimity
  Berlioz's view of, 36–38, 43–44,
  48–55, 58–59, 74–76

heard in the *Requiem*, 45–46, 48,
  51–55, 59–65, 66–76, 106–8
as referential, 53–55
and the sacred, 36–38, 55–60,
  62–65, 66–76, 106–8
as sensory experience, 48–51,
  56–57, 59–60
theories of, 46–50, 53–57

Te Deum (Berlioz), 3–6, 104–5
Théâtre du Châtelet, 93–94, 97–98
theatricality, trope of, 6–7, 60–61,
  101–6
Thiers, Adolphe, 35–36
Tiersot, Julien, 104–5
T.M. (critic), 93–94
Tommasini, Anthony, 103
Toulmon, Bottée de. *See* Bottée de
  Toulmon, Auguste
Tuileries Chapel (Chapelle royale),
  31–33

Verdi, Giuseppe, 105–6

X. Y. Z. (critic), 16–18, 25–27

Yates, Devoe, 4–6

The manufacturer's authorised representative in the EU for product safety is Oxford
University Press España S.A. of El Parque Empresarial San Fernando de Henares,
Avenida de Castilla, 2 – 28830 Madrid (www.oup.es/en or product.safety@oup.com).
OUP España S.A. also acts as importer into Spain of products made by the manufacturer.

Printed in the USA/Agawam, MA
June 27, 2025

889683.001